2019–2021 JOINT LEARNING REPORT ON THE IMPLEMENTATION OF THE ACCOUNTABILITY MECHANISM POLICY

ACCOUNTABILITY MECHANISM STRENGTHENS GOOD GOVERNANCE

SEPTEMBER 2023

ASIAN DEVELOPMENT BANK

ADB

Note:
In this publication, "$" refers to United States dollars.

On the cover: The cover shows that progress and people are at the heart of ADB's Accountability Mechanism's mission to empower communities, address grievances, and pave the way for sustainable change.

Cover design by Cleone Baradas.

Contents

Figures and Boxes

Abbreviations

ADB	Asian Development Bank
AMP	Accountability Mechanism Policy
CCSD	Climate Change and Sustainable Development Department
CRP	Compliance Review Panel
DMC	developing member country
ESS	environmental and social policy standards
GRM	grievance redress mechanism
IAM	Independent Accountability Mechanism
IED	Independent Evaluation Department
IFI	international financial institution
ISMS	Integrated Safeguards Management System
MDB	multilateral development bank
OCRP	Office of the Compliance Review Panel
OSPF	Office of the Special Project Facilitator
SPF	special project facilitator
SPS	Safeguard Policy Statement
TA	technical assistance

A stretch of road covered by the Sri Lanka Southern Transport Development Project (STDP). The STDP supports a twofold primary objective of spurring economic development in the region and significantly reducing the rate of road accidents (photo by ADB).

Executive Summary

This joint learning report focuses on the theme that the Asian Development Bank (ADB) Accountability Mechanism strengthens good governance. The twin functions of the ADB Accountability Mechanism—compliance review and problem solving—act as pillars that support and strengthen good governance. The ADB Accountability Mechanism bolsters eight characteristics of good governance: (i) participatory, (ii) consensus-oriented, (iii) accountable, (iv) transparent, (v) responsive, (vi) effective and efficient, (vii) equitable and inclusive, and (viii) follows the rule of law. The Accountability Mechanism holds these building blocks together to strengthen the structure of good governance. The lessons learned from 2019 to 2021 are viewed through the lens of good governance.

This learning report begins with an analysis of the causes—or triggers—for filing Accountability Mechanism complaints. The analysis reveals the trends of the triggers that called for the application of the mechanism. These triggers signify instances when gaps in good governance may have occurred, when opportunities for reinforcing good governance are present, and which can point to measures that may be taken to strengthen good governance.

The second part of the analysis considers the lessons learned—distilled by the Accountability Mechanism offices—through the lens of good governance. The analysis intends to demonstrate how good governance is strengthened through the application of the lessons learned.

Further analysis examines several recurring and emerging issues that have a two-way interaction with good governance. Retaliation or reprisal risk and the lack of access to effective remedies can dissuade participation in the Accountability Mechanism and hinder good governance and development effectiveness. The handling and tracking of complaints are examined as essential to transparency, responsiveness, and accountability. This report briefly discusses an ongoing update of the ADB 2009 Safeguard Policy Statement, which is expected to further strengthen good governance.

This report revisits recommendations made in the 2018 Joint Learning Report (2016–2018) and is based on a thorough analysis of all aspects and triggers. It makes recommendations for some possible reforms in the context that the Accountability Mechanism strengthens good governance through

(i)   due diligence criteria with standardized and tailored components to capture both risks that are common to the industry and that are unique to the project;

(ii)   guidelines on the progressive escalation of issues within ADB to ensure the effective implementation of remedies;

(iii)   vigilant enforcement of specific time frames for completion of due diligence;

(iv)   internal guidance on human resource and financial governance in safeguards compliance, patterned after financial planning and cost management in project activities;

(v)   development of retaliation risk guidelines and assessment tools safeguarding people bringing complaints under ADB-financed projects;

(vi)   strengthened environmental and social protection provisions under the Environmental and Social Framework, 2016 (as amended 2019) with detailed project implementation guidelines for human rights considerations;

(vii)   strengthened participation and meaningful consultation;

(viii)   strengthening efforts to improve grievance redress mechanisms; and

(ix)   establishing an ADB-wide complaint management and risk management system.

Introduction: Good Governance, ADB, and Its Core Values

The Asian Development Bank (ADB) Accountability Mechanism Policy (AMP) 2012 is designed to (i) increase ADB development effectiveness and project quality; (ii) be responsive to the concerns of project-affected people and fair to all stakeholders; (iii) reflect the highest professional and technical standards in its staffing and operations; (iv) be as independent and transparent as possible; (v) be cost-effective and efficient; and (vi) be complementary to other supervision, audit, quality control, and evaluation systems at ADB. These objectives intersect with many elements of good governance.

While literature defines the concept of good governance with some variation, the substance bears significant similarities. For instance, the eight major characteristics of good governance are identified as (i) participatory, (ii) consensus-oriented, (iii) accountable, (iv) transparent, (v) responsive, (vi) effective and efficient, (vii) equitable and inclusive, and (viii) follows the rule of law.[1] Good governance is also considered to be underpinned by openness, participation, accountability, effectiveness, and coherence.[2] Good governance encompasses ensuring the rule of law, improving the efficiency and accountability of both the public and the private sectors, and tackling corruption.[3] It includes the elements of accountability, transparency, combating corruption, participation, and legal and judicial frameworks.[4] For this joint learning report, the eight listed major characteristics of good governance—which may encapsulate many of the characteristics described in related literature—will be used as a starting point.

The accountability of multilateral development banks (MDBs) is grounded on the rationale of ensuring good governance of the institutions that enjoy immunities and privileges, and this joint learning report focuses on the theme that the ADB Accountability Mechanism strengthens good governance. To ensure good governance and enhance development effectiveness, ADB has initiated a transformation exercise by defining its core values to be "client-centric," "trustworthy," and "transformational."[5] This cultural transformation is recognized in the ADB New Operating Model.[6]

The ADB Accountability Mechanism has been a prime example of these core values since its inception. The mechanism is designed to maximize the development effectiveness of ADB work

---

[1] The eight characteristics of good governance are adopted from a United Nations Economic and Social Commission for Asia and the Pacific (UNESCAP) paper that may encapsulate definitions of good governance from several sources: UNESCAP. 2009. *What is Good Governance?* Bangkok.

[2] European Commission. 2001. *European Governance: A White Paper.* Brussels.

[3] International Monetary Fund. 1997. *Good Governance: The IMF's Role.* Washington, DC.

[4] African Development Bank. 1999. *Bank Group Policy on Good Governance.*

[5] Independent Evaluation Department. 2022. *One ADB: An Evaluation of ADB's Approach to Delivering Strategy 2030.* Manila: ADB.

[6] ADB. 2022. *Organizational Review: A New Operating Model to Accelerate ADB's Transformation Toward Strategy 2030 and Beyond.* Manila.

by listening to the unheard (affected persons) and responding to their issues (client-centric), and building transparency, integrity, and honesty along the way (trustworthy). Its work focuses on accountability, which is essentially learning from mistakes to do better for the optimum development impact (transformational). In so doing, the ADB Accountability Mechanism reinforces all the eight characteristics of good governance.

The compliance review function, performed by the Compliance Review Panel (CRP), and the problem-solving function, performed by the special project facilitator (SPF)—which together make up the Accountability Mechanism in ADB—can be taken as one of the pillars that support and strengthen good governance. The mechanism by which the ADB Accountability Mechanism strengthens good governance is illustrated by the metaphor of pillars supporting the building blocks (or characteristics) of good governance (Figure 1).

Figure 1: Characteristics of Good Governance

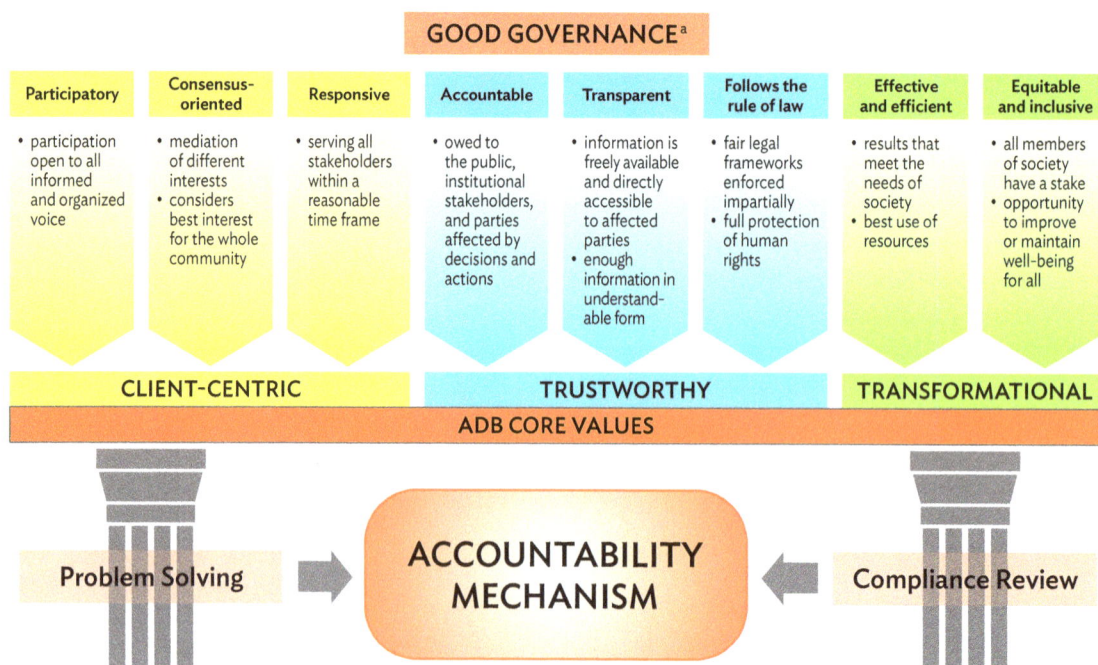

GOOD GOVERNANCE[a]

Participatory	Consensus-oriented	Responsive	Accountable	Transparent	Follows the rule of law	Effective and efficient	Equitable and inclusive
• participation open to all informed and organized voice	• mediation of different interests • considers best interest for the whole community	• serving all stakeholders within a reasonable time frame	• owed to the public, institutional stakeholders, and parties affected by decisions and actions	• information is freely available and directly accessible to affected parties • enough information in understand-able form	• fair legal frameworks enforced impartially • full protection of human rights	• results that meet the needs of society • best use of resources	• all members of society have a stake • opportunity to improve or maintain well-being for all

CLIENT-CENTRIC   TRUSTWORTHY   TRANSFORMATIONAL

ADB CORE VALUES

Problem Solving → ACCOUNTABILITY MECHANISM ← Compliance Review

a   Characteristics of good governance based on the UNESCAP definition (What Is Good Governance?). ADB interfaces with a number (but not all) of these characteristics.

Source: The eight characteristics of good governance are adopted from a United Nations Economic and Social Commission for Asia and the Pacific (UNESCAP) paper which may encapsulate definitions of good governance from several sources: UNESCAP. 2009. *What is Good Governance?* Bangkok.

Purpose and Methodology of This Report

The 2022 Joint Learning Report was prepared by the Office of the Compliance Review Panel (OCRP), the Office of the Special Project Facilitator (OSPF), the Climate Change and Sustainable Development Department (CCSD, formerly the Sustainable Development and Climate Change Department), and the Independent Evaluation Department (IED) by distilling ADB experiences, insights, and lessons. Complaints before 2019 for long-standing and recurring issues and after 2021 for emerging issues are also considered. The learning report analyzes the triggers for the complaints filed during 2019–2021, as well as previous complaints which were the subject of the lessons learned reports published by the OCRP and SPF during the same time frame.

The examination of triggers establishes trends when the application of the ADB Accountability Mechanism was necessary. These triggers signify when gaps in good governance may have occurred. The triggers also point to opportunities for reinforcing good governance. The outcome of the analysis of triggers and lessons learned are recommendations for possible reforms and the reinforcement of recommendations in past joint learning reports that have not yet been implemented.

Workers at the Georgia Sustainable Urban Transport Investment Program (SUTIP), Tranche 3. The third project of the SUTIP is aimed at improving the urban environment and strengthening economic and tourism development, as well as regional integration (photo by ADB).

Overview of Complaints Reaching the Accountability Mechanism

As a prelude to the analysis in this joint learning report, this section looks into data on Accountability Mechanism complaints filed from 2019 to 2021, which are juxtaposed against data from 2016 to 2018.[7]

Total Complaints Lodged

During 2016–2018, 88 complaints were lodged with the Accountability Mechanism. Of these, 10 were forwarded to the CRP and 29 to the SPF. The complaint receiving officer had 49 complaints initially pending but based on a Memorandum dated 30 August 2019 submitted by the OCRP and OSPF to the Office of the General Counsel, the same 49 complaints were deemed closed for failure to complete the minimum requirements for filing a complaint.

During 2019–2021, 104 complaints were lodged with the Accountability Mechanism (Figure 2). Of these, 3 were forwarded to the CRP and 40 to the SPF. There were 56 complaints closed for failure to complete the minimum requirements for filing a complaint.

Complaints lodged with the Accountability Mechanism during 2019–2021 increased in number compared to 2016–2018. This may reflect an increased awareness of the mechanism, as well as an improved perception of its efficacy.

A majority of the complaints requested problem solving, increasing from 29 to 40 compared to the previous period. This may indicate that stakeholders—particularly affected persons—preferred the informal, flexible, and consensus-based methods of resolving issues through the OSPF.

---

[7]   Figures are from the 2018 Learning Report on Implementation of the Accountability Mechanism Policy, the 2019, 2020, and 2021 Accountability Mechanism Annual Reports, and the complaints receiving officer.

Figure 2: Total Complaints Lodged with the Accountability Mechanism, 2019–2021

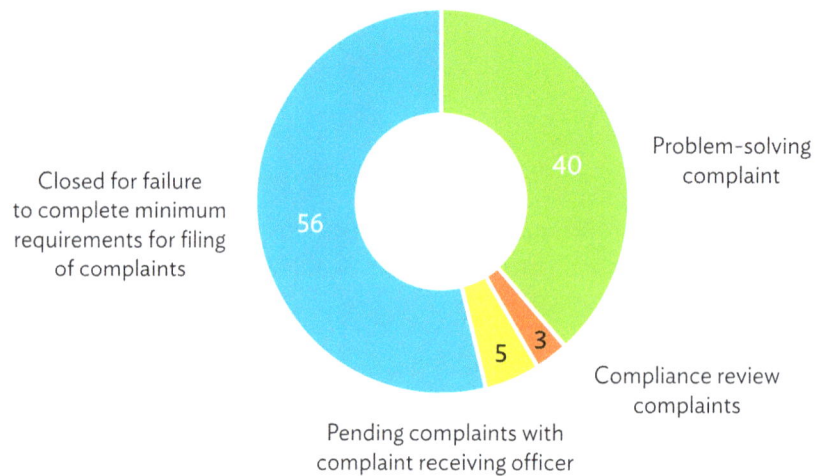

Closed for failure
to complete minimum
requirements for filing
of complaints

56

Problem-solving
complaint

40

5   3

Compliance review
complaints

Pending complaints with
complaint receiving officer

Note: "Closed" refers to complaints closed by the complaint receiving officer as the complainants were unable to complete the minimum requirements for filing a complaint, particularly the information required by para. 151 of the 2012 Accountability Mechanism Policy.[a] Such closure of complaints is different from closure after problem solving or after compliance review is completed, which data was not tracked in this report or the 2016–2018 report.

Source: Compiled from ADB Accountability Mechanism Annual Reports 2019, 2020, and 2021. Compared with ADB 2016 to 2018 data, 2018 Learning Report on Implementation of the Accountability Mechanism Policy (Figure 2, p. 7).

_____

[a] This information includes: (i) names, designations, addresses, and contact information of the complainants and their representative; (ii) if a complaint is made through a representative, identification of the project-affected people on whose behalf the complaint is made and evidence of the authority to represent them; (iii) whether the complainants choose to keep their identities confidential; (iv) whether the complainants choose to undergo problem solving with the OSPF or compliance review with the CRP; (v) a brief description of the ADB-assisted project, including the name and location; (vi) a description of the direct and material harm that has been, or is likely to be, caused to the complainants by the ADB-assisted project; (vii) a description of the complainants' good faith efforts to address the problems first with the operations department concerned, and the results of these efforts; and (viii) if applicable, a description of the complainants' efforts to address the complaint with the OSPF, and the results of these efforts.

Breakdown of Complaints Lodged

Six problem-solving complaints were filed in 2016, 12 in 2017, and 11 in 2018. Problem-solving complaints increased when 12 complaints were filed in 2019, 11 in 2020, and 17 in 2021.

Four compliance review complaints were filed in 2016, three in 2017, and three in 2018. This is significantly higher than the succeeding period which saw the filing of two complaints in 2019, none in 2020, and one in 2021.

The complaint receiving officer had 10 complaints pending (before being forwarded to the SPF or CRP) in 2016, 12 in 2017, and 11 in 2018. This contrasts with zero complaints pending in 2019, three in 2020, and two in 2021 (Figure 3). The complaints during 2016–2018 were eventually deemed closed under the Office of the General Counsel Memorandum of 30 August 2019.

Figure 3: Breakdown of Complaints Lodged with the Accountability Mechanism, 2019–2021

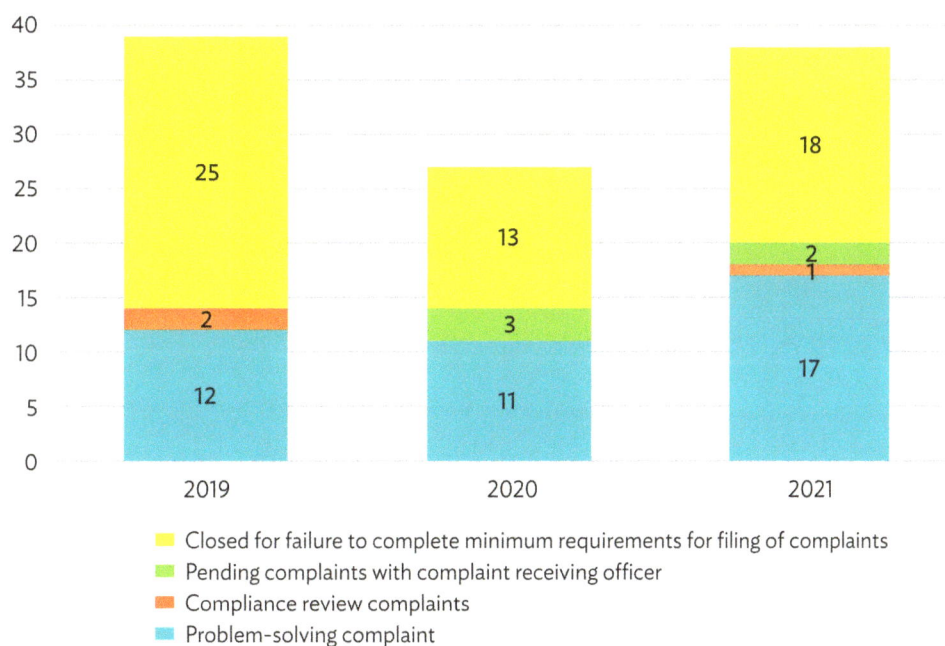

Legend:
- Closed for failure to complete minimum requirements for filing of complaints
- Pending complaints with complaint receiving officer
- Compliance review complaints
- Problem-solving complaint

Source: Compiled from ADB Accountability Mechanism Annual Reports 2019, 2020, and 2021. Compared with ADB 2016 to 2018 data, 2018 Learning Report on Implementation of the Accountability Mechanism Policy (Figure 3 p. 7).

There was an increasing trend of complaints filed in 2016 (20), 2017 (29), and 2018 (39), while the trend started to plateau at 39 in 2019. However, the trend may have been affected by the coronavirus disease (COVID-19) pandemic in 2020 where the data show a decrease at 27, although it increased again in 2021 to 38.

Projects with More Than One Complaint

During 2016–2018, 15 projects had more than one complaint, compared to 20 projects during 2019–2021. The highest number of complaints in a single project reached 10 during 2016–2018, while the highest during 2019–2021 was 6 (Figure 4).

Figure 4: Projects with More Than One Complaint, 2019–2021

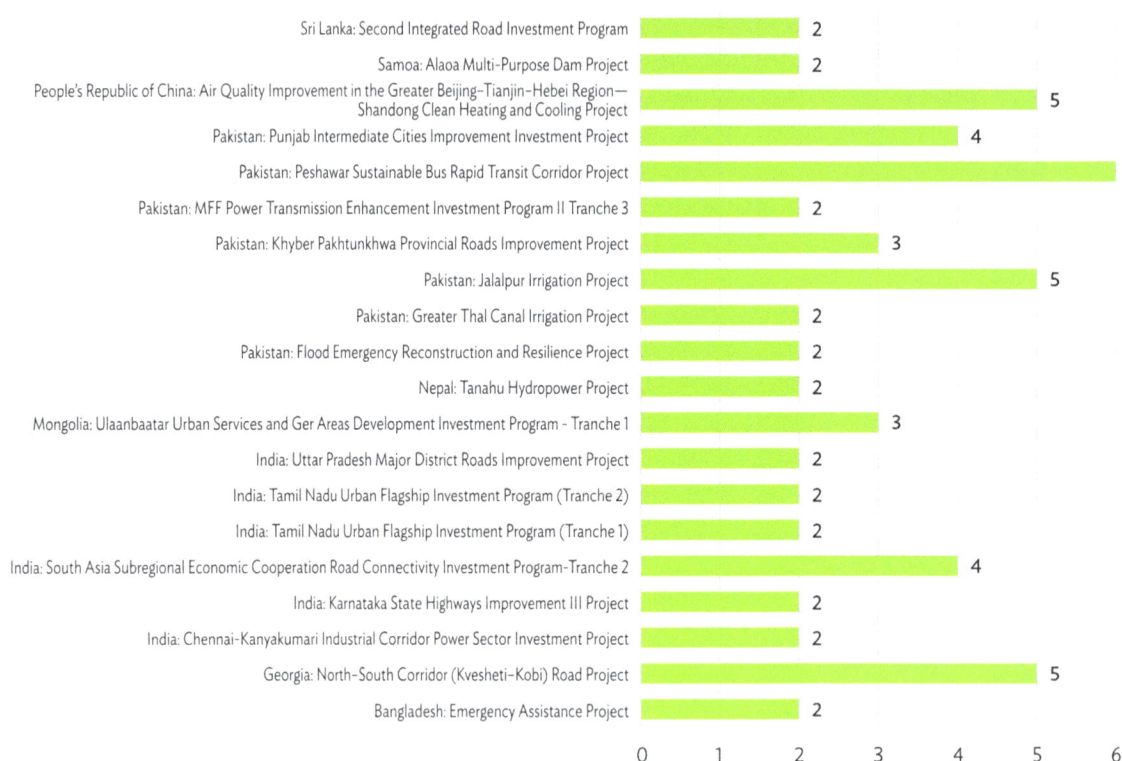

Project	Complaints
Sri Lanka: Second Integrated Road Investment Program	2
Samoa: Alaoa Multi-Purpose Dam Project	2
People's Republic of China: Air Quality Improvement in the Greater Beijing–Tianjin–Hebei Region—Shandong Clean Heating and Cooling Project	5
Pakistan: Punjab Intermediate Cities Improvement Investment Project	4
Pakistan: Peshawar Sustainable Bus Rapid Transit Corridor Project	6
Pakistan: MFF Power Transmission Enhancement Investment Program II Tranche 3	2
Pakistan: Khyber Pakhtunkhwa Provincial Roads Improvement Project	3
Pakistan: Jalalpur Irrigation Project	5
Pakistan: Greater Thal Canal Irrigation Project	2
Pakistan: Flood Emergency Reconstruction and Resilience Project	2
Nepal: Tanahu Hydropower Project	2
Mongolia: Ulaanbaatar Urban Services and Ger Areas Development Investment Program - Tranche 1	3
India: Uttar Pradesh Major District Roads Improvement Project	2
India: Tamil Nadu Urban Flagship Investment Program (Tranche 2)	2
India: Tamil Nadu Urban Flagship Investment Program (Tranche 1)	2
India: South Asia Subregional Economic Cooperation Road Connectivity Investment Program-Tranche 2	4
India: Karnataka State Highways Improvement III Project	2
India: Chennai-Kanyakumari Industrial Corridor Power Sector Investment Project	2
Georgia: North–South Corridor (Kvesheti–Kobi) Road Project	5
Bangladesh: Emergency Assistance Project	2

Source: Compiled from ADB Accountability Mechanism Annual Reports 2019, 2020, and 2021. Compared with ADB 2016 to 2018 data, 2018 earning Report on Implementation of the Accountability Mechanism Policy (Figure 5, p. 8).

The number of projects with more than one complaint increased from 15 projects during 2016–2018 to 20 projects during 2019–2021. The number of complaints per project also appeared to increase during this period, with more projects having at least three complaints.

Total Complaints by Sector

The highest number of complaints by sector was transport, followed by water and other urban infrastructure and services, and energy. However, a broader range of sectors is represented, including finance, education, industry and trade, and information and communication technology (Figure 5).

Figure 5: Total Complaints by Sector, 2019–2021

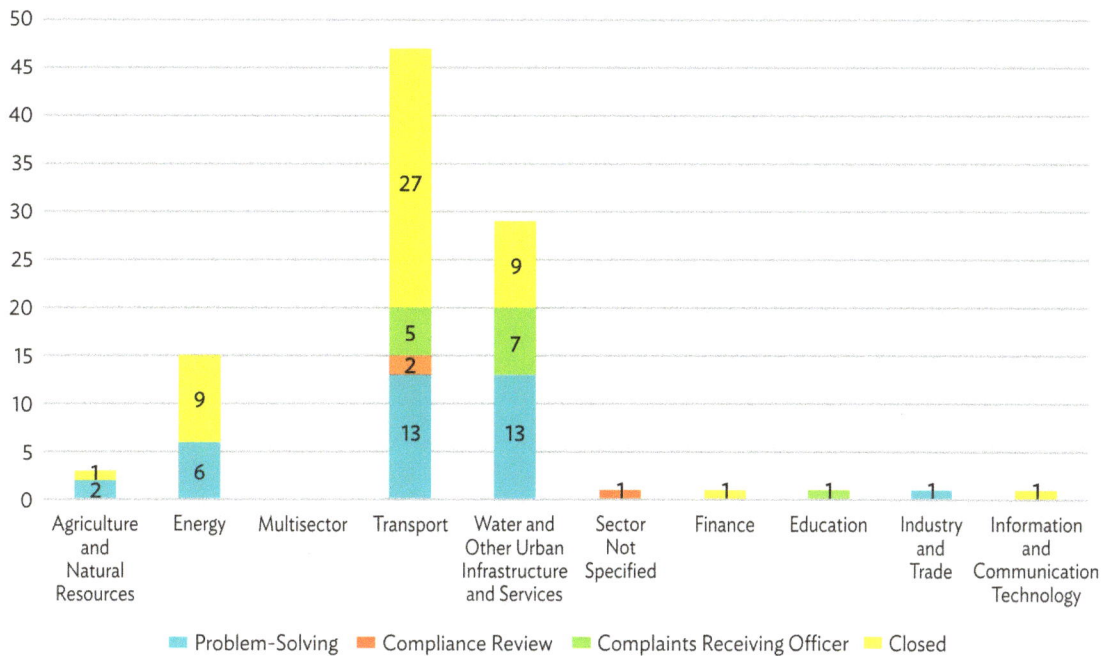

Source: ADB Accountability Mechanism Annual Reports 2019, 2020, and 2021. Compared with ADB 2016 to 2018 data, 2018 Learning Report on Implementation of the Accountability Mechanism Policy (Figure 6, p. 8).

On balance, trends during 2019–2021 remained consistent with those during 2016–2018.

Triggers and Lessons Learned: Trends Analysis of Issues That Trigger the Filing of Accountability Mechanism Complaints

This joint learning report identifies triggers for complaints filed under the Accountability Mechanism during 2019–2021. Certain recurring and emerging issues in complaints outside this period, as well as the Accountability Mechanism Lessons Learned Report series during 2019–2021 (Box 1 and Box 2), are also included in the analysis.

continued on next page

Box 1 *continued*

Georgia Sustainable Urban Transport Investment Program, Tranche 3 (Georgia Sustainable Urban Transport Project)
Request No. 2016/1
OCRP Lessons Learned
OSPF Lessons Learned

Mongolia Ulaanbaatar Urban Services and Ger Areas Development Investment Program, Tranche 1 (Mongolia Ulaanbaatar GADIP)
Complaint, SPF-2018-05
Lessons Learned Report

OSPF = Office of the Special Project Facilitator, OCRP = Office of the Compliance Review Panel, SPF = special project facilitator.

Box 2
Additional Complaints/Lessons Learned Reports Considered

Viet Nam Central Mekong Delta Region Connectivity Project (Viet Nam CMDRCP)
Lessons Learned Report

Sri Lanka Integrated Road Investment Program (Sri Lanka iRoad Program)
Lessons Learned Report

Cambodia Rehabilitation of the Railway Project (Cambodia Railway Project)
Request No. 2012/2
Lessons Learned Report

continued on next page

Box 2 *continued*

Indonesia Integrated Citarum Water Resources Management Investment Program Project 1 (Indonesia Citarum Water Project)
Request No. 2012/1
Lessons Learned Report

Kyrgyz Republic: Central Asia Regional Economic Cooperation Transport Corridor 1 (Bishkek-Torugart Road) Project 1 (CAREC Transport Project)
Request No. 2011/2
Lessons Learned Report

Fuzhou Environmental Improvement Project in the People's Republic of China (PRC Fuzhou Environmental Improvement Project)
Request No. 2009/1
Lessons Learned Report

Philippines Visayas Base-Load Power Development Project (Philippines Visayas Power Project)
Request No. 2011/1
Lessons Learned Report

Sri Lanka Southern Transport Development Project (Sri Lanka Transport Development Project)
Request No. 2004/1
Lesson Learned Report

PRC = People's Republic of China.

Examining common triggers observed from an analysis of the complaints provided an overview of the lessons learned. The lessons learned are then viewed from the perspective of good governance. The trends analysis of the lessons will be useful for ADB in aligning its operations with its core values and ensuring good governance.

Trends Analysis of Common Triggers

Complaints were filed under the ADB Accountability Mechanism for reasons ranging from inadequate compensation to inadequate consultation and information dissemination, problematic resettlement sites, and environmental damage.

Although all triggers may result or are likely to result in harming the affected persons, this report—for discussion—classified these triggers into two groups: adverse impact trigger and procedural non-adherence trigger. Both triggers may overlap; for example, procedural non-adherence triggers lead to adverse impacts and hence cause harm.

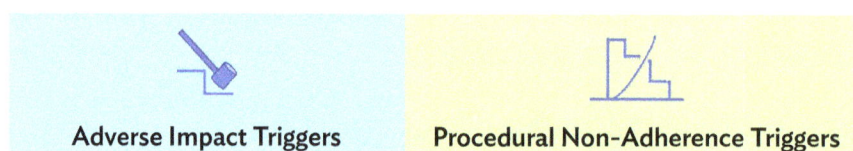

Adverse Impact Triggers   **Procedural Non-Adherence Triggers**

Adverse impact triggers refer to harm directly suffered by the affected persons due to a project. Procedural non-adherence triggers refer to the failure of ADB to comply with its policies and safeguards during project design, processing, or implementation, which could subsequently result in adverse impacts on affected persons.

Adverse impact triggers and procedural non-adherence triggers are dealt with separately. Adverse impact triggers may be addressed with an immediate response or short-term action, but procedural non-adherence triggers often warrant systemic changes to ensure such noncompliance is not repeated. As a result, adverse impacts and complaints based on such triggers are addressed with an institutional response through a systemic improvement.

Adverse impact and procedural non-adherence triggers may cover the following areas (Box 3):

Box 3

Adverse Impact and Procedural Non-Adherence Triggers

Adverse Impact Triggers	Procedural Non-Adherence Triggers
(i) involuntary resettlement issues	(i) lack of transparency
(ii) damage to property	(ii) grievance redress mechanism concerns
(iii) loss or impairment of livelihood	(iii) other broad safeguards and policies concerns
(iv) damage to the environment	(iv) impact assessment concerns
(v) risk to life, safety, health, or well-being	

Box 4 provides some examples of adverse impact triggers:

Box 4

Adverse Impact Triggers

Involuntary Resettlement Issues

- Disputes on valuation rate for compensation (e.g., *Georgia Batumi Bypass Road Project, Mongolia Ulaanbaatar GADIP*)
- The remoteness of, and inadequate basic services in, a resettlement site (e.g., *Cambodia Railway Project*)
- Loss of homes (e.g., *Sri Lanka Transport Development Project*)
- Dispersion of integrated communities (e.g., *Sri Lanka Transport Development Project*)

Damage to Property

- Damage to houses, graves, cofferdams, water supply lines, temples, and other structures (e.g., *Mongolia Ulaanbaatar GADIP, Georgia Batumi Bypass Road Project, Georgia Sustainable Urban Transport Project, Sri Lanka iRoad Program, Sri Lanka Transport Development Project*)
- Flooding due to dysfunctional culverts or blocked drainage (e.g., *Sri Lanka iRoad Program, Viet Nam CMDRCP*)
- Impaired use of land (e.g., *Sri Lanka Clean Energy Project*)
- Damage to trees (e.g., *Georgia Sustainable Urban Transport Project, CAREC Transport Project*)

Loss or Impairment of Livelihood

- Damage to business premises (e.g., Sri Lanka iRoad Program)
- Inability to pay the business loan (e.g., *Sri Lanka Clean Energy Project*)
- Insufficient compensation for income losses (e.g., *Cambodia Railway Project, Mongolia Ulaanbaatar GADIP*)
- Impoverishment (e.g., *Cambodia Railway Project*)
- Inaccessibility of fishing grounds (e.g., *India Mundra Power Project*)
- Lack of employment opportunities (e.g., *India Mundra Power Project*)
- Loss of timber and fruit trees (e.g., *Sri Lanka Clean Energy Project*)

Damage to the Environment

- Air, water, and thermal pollution (e.g., *Sri Lanka iRoad Program, India Mundra Power Project, Philippines Visayas Power Project*)
- Degradation of wetlands (e.g., *Sri Lanka Transport Development Project*)
- A decline in the groundwater table (e.g., *India Mundra Power Project*)

Risk to Life, Safety, Health, or Well-Being

- Violation of rights (e.g., right to adequate housing, right to affordable and adequate water supply; right of children to an adequate standard of living (physical, mental, spiritual, moral, and social development); right to enjoyment of the highest attainable standard of health; right to education based on equal opportunity; and the right to an effective remedy (e.g., *Cambodia Railway Project*)
- Incidence of violence against women (e.g., *India Mundra Power Project*)
- Health risks (e.g., *Philippines Visayas Power Project, India Mundra Power Project*)

Source: Box 1 and Box 2.

Box 5 provides some samples of procedural non-adherence triggers.

Box 5
Procedural Non-Adherence Triggers

Lack of Transparency
- Failure to communicate adequate project information (for instance, requirements for compensation, entitlement matrix, computation of compensation) (e.g., *Georgia Sustainable Urban Transport Project, Georgia Batumi Bypass Road Project, Mongolia Ulaanbaatar GADIP, Cambodia Railway Project*)
- Lack of meaningful consultation (e.g., *Georgia Batumi Bypass Road Project, Georgia Sustainable Urban Transport Project, India Mundra Power Project*)
- Land and property appraisal and valuation in the absence of key family members (e.g., *Mongolia Ulaanbaatar GADIP*)
- Unanticipated and undisclosed design or scope changes (e.g., *Mongolia Ulaanbaatar Urban Services Investment Program, CAREC Transport Project*)
- Inadequate information and consultation during the preparation of the resettlement plan (e.g., *Fuzhou Environmental Improvement Project*)

Grievance Redress Mechanism (GRM) concerns
- Inability of GRM to deal with the complaint in a timely and transparent manner (e.g., *Georgia Batumi Bypass Road Project*)
- Lack of standard procedure for handling complaints (e.g., *Georgia Sustainable Urban Transport Project*)
- Inadequate grievance redress during project implementation (e.g., *Cambodia Railway Project*)

Impact Assessment Concerns
- Inadequate assessment of social and environmental impacts (e.g., *CAREC Transport Project*)
- Failure to verify economic and environmental data (e.g., *Philippines Visayas Power Project, Cambodia Railway Project*)
- Inadequate identification of affected persons (e.g., *Georgia Sustainable Urban Transport Project, India Mundra Power Project*)

Other Broad Safeguards and Policies Concerns
- Failure to comply with ADB involuntary resettlement requirements (e.g., *CAREC Transport Project*)
- Failure to adhere to environmental and social policies (e.g., *Batumi Bypass Road Project, Georgia Sustainable Urban Transport Project, Sri Lanka Transport Development Project*)
- Lack of knowledge of stakeholders on Safeguard Policy Statement (e.g., *CAREC Transport Project*)

Source: Box 1 and Box 2.

Triggers Are Cracks in the Structure of Good Governance

Complaint triggers signal structural weaknesses in implementation processes for development projects and the policies intended to maximize the effectiveness of these projects. In a sense, these triggers are cracks in the system leading to compromised governance if not addressed.

To illustrate:

Complaint triggers such as

- (i)   resettlement issues;
- (ii)   damage to property;
- (iii) loss or impairment of livelihood;
- (iv) damage to the environment; and
- (v)   risk to life, safety, health, or well-being

have underlying issues of

- (i)   lack of participation due to affected persons' concerns being left unheard,
- (ii)   lack of importance given to consensus such that inputs and feedback were not adequately considered, and
- (iii) lack of transparency which produced inadequate information and triggered fears among the affected persons.

Almost **all types of complaint triggers** encountered in the ADB Accountability Mechanism may also have underlying issues of lack of

- (i)   **responsiveness**, such that concerns and grievances of affected persons appear unaddressed; and
- (ii)   **effectiveness and efficiency** are manifested by inaction or failure to utilize resources that leads to the failure to meet the needs of affected persons.

These good governance characteristics could otherwise ensure results and appropriate remedies according to the needs of the stakeholders—within a reasonable time frame—and subsequently lower the risk of grievances and complaints being escalated.

Complaint triggers under **lack of transparency** may be directly traced to the absence or deficiencies in **participation, consensus orientation,** and **transparency**.

Procedural gap triggers include a lack of transparency, and issues with the grievance redress mechanism (GRM), ADB safeguards and policies, and impact assessments. These are directly related to shortcomings in adherence to the applicable policies and standards and the rule of law and could be avoided through the provision of detailed guidelines, the observance of such guidelines, rules and regulations, standards, and ADB safeguards and policies.

If such triggers recur in several projects, the problem or inadequacy may be systemic. ADB should promptly resolve the systemic problem or inadequacy since it can result in significant inefficiencies during project implementation through (i) increased project costs, (ii) delayed project implementation, (iii) additional resource and workforce requirements to implement remedies, and (iv) stakeholder resistance due to possible recurrence of issues and/or grievances. The repeated or prolonged incidence of such problems and inadequacies can seriously undermine good governance and impair development effectiveness (Figure 6).

Figure 6: Results of Systemic Impact Triggers

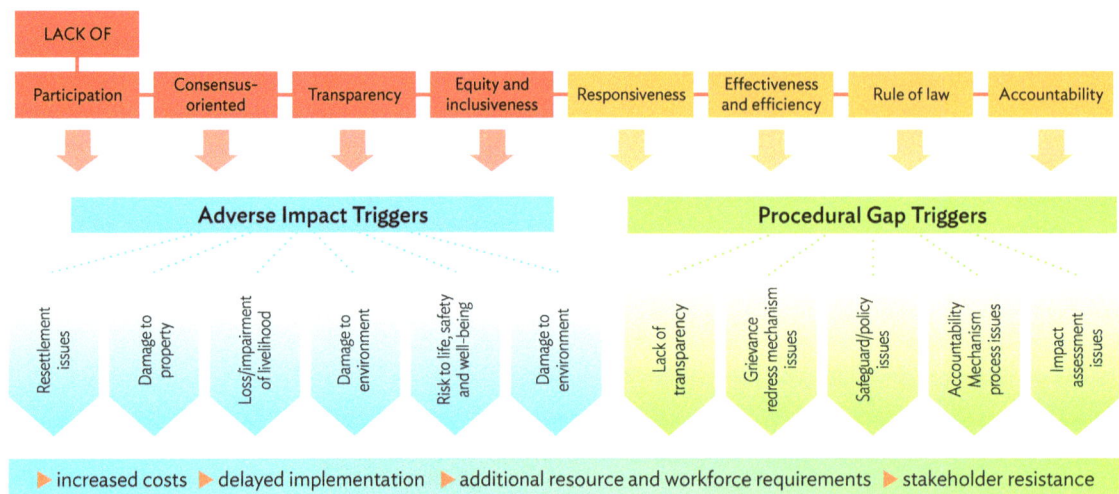

Source: The eight characteristics of good governance are adopted from a United Nations Economic and Social Commission for Asia and the Pacific (UNESCAP) paper which may encapsulate definitions of good governance from several sources: UNESCAP. 2009. *What is Good Governance?* Bangkok.

Building Structural Strength: Strengthening Good Governance through Accountability Mechanism Lessons

From 2018 to 2021, both the OSPF and OCRP published various lessons learned reports based on complaints that their offices have handled since 2003. This process indicated that there is a trend of repetitive triggers that lead to complaints and that a systemic change to strengthen development effectiveness is needed. Addressing some of these lessons will ensure (i) strengthened governance of ADB internal systems and processes; (ii) strengthened cooperation and governance capacity of implementing partners at the borrower level; and (iii) strengthened supervision, monitoring, and reviewing the capacity of ADB staff resulting in well-governed projects.

The linkage between the lessons learned and the most-used eight characteristics of good governance gives a perspective of how the Accountability Mechanism serves as an ADB partner in ensuring and achieving good governance.

PARTICIPATORY

Participation—whether directly or through legitimate intermediate institutions or representatives—is a cornerstone of good governance.[8] It must entail wide participation "from conception to implementation."[9] Through participation, "stakeholders exercise influence over public policy decisions, and share control over resources and institutions that affect their lives."[10]

In ADB-assisted operations, participation "refers to the processes through which stakeholders influence or contribute to designing, implementing, and monitoring a development activity."[11] ADB also views participation not as a goal in itself, but as something that helps achieve improved development results. It is said that "by ensuring stakeholders understand and can participate in the decisions, resource allocations, and activities that affect their lives, it ensures attainment of the benefits from this engagement."[12]

[8] UNESCAP. 2009. *What is Good Governance?* Bangkok: p. 2.
[9] European Commission. 2001. *European Governance: A White Paper*. Brussels.
[10] African Development Bank. 1999. *Bank Group Policy on Good Governance*, p. 3.
[11] ADB. 2012. *Strengthening Participation for Development Results: An Asian Development Bank Guide to Participation*. Manila, p. 2.
[12] Footnote 11.

CONSENSUS-ORIENTED

Good governance requires the mediation of different interests in society to reach a broad consensus of best interests of the whole community and how this can be achieved.[13] It also requires a broad and long-term perspective on what is needed for sustainable human development and how to achieve the goals of such development.[14]

ADB experience illustrates how the Accountability Mechanism helps promote consensus by consensus-based problem solving through an agreed course of action, and through remedial actions that are considered fair by all parties. This way, the concerns of all are heard, consistent with the philosophy that there be "no one left behind" in development efforts.

TRANSPARENT

Transparency is broadly defined as public access to knowledge of the policies and strategies of government, particularly to those who will be affected by decisions made and enforced.[15] In a more practical sense, transparency means that decisions taken and their enforcement are done in a manner that follows rules and regulations. It also requires that enough information is provided and that it is provided in easily understandable forms and media.[16]

Within ADB, transparency—such as embodied in its Access to Information Policy—promotes stakeholder trust and increases development impact.

Related Lessons

Meaningful stakeholder engagement:

(i)   contributes directly to the participatory, inclusive, consultative, and transparent nature of governance. This entails meaningful consultation where feedback from stakeholders is taken into consideration, heard, and—where appropriate—integrated into the project design (e.g., Georgia Sustainable Urban Transport Project, Sri Lanka CENEIP);

(ii)   entails providing sufficient information about the project, compensation entitlements, and similar matters to prevent unfounded fears and grievances (e.g., Georgia Sustainable Urban Transport Project, Mongolia Ulaanbaatar GADIP);

(iii)   contributes to community support for the project since it builds a sense of community ownership, such as the involvement of local community officials in problem-solving processes (e.g., Sri Lanka iRoad Program);

---

[13]   Footnote 8.
[14]   Footnote 8.
[15]   African Development Bank. 1999. *Bank Group Policy on Good Governance.*
[16]   Footnote 8.

(iv) reinforces participation and consensus during the grievance resolution process since most grievances cannot be resolved in isolation by a single party but requires the participation and intervention of various stakeholders, and their commitment to resource allocations (e.g., Sri Lanka iRoad Program);

(v)   minimizes grievances that arise later in the project and enhances the ability to efficiently resolve problems (e.g., Georgia Batumi Bypass Road Project, Sri Lanka iRoad Program) as strong and functional project-level GRMs can help affected persons feel heard, as well as alert executing agencies or ADB operations departments about issues or problems at an early stage;

(vi) may prevent seeking redress from unwarranted venues that can cause potential disruptions to project implementation, particularly awareness-raising regarding the GRM (e.g., Sri Lanka iRoad Program, Mongolia Ulaanbaatar GADIP);

(vii) can result in the reduction of harm to potentially affected persons since their concerns can be considered promptly (e.g., Philippines Visayas Base-Load Power Project); and

(viii) can improve project compliance when stakeholders can understand their roles in compliance and its demands through effective awareness-raising and capacity-building activities (e.g., Mongolia Ulaanbaatar GADIP).

RULE OF LAW IN THE FORM OF ADHERENCE TO POLICIES AND SAFEGUARDS

Good governance requires respect for the rule of law where fair legal frameworks are enforced impartially.[17]

Within ADB, the rule of law can be approximated by adherence by ADB to its policies, procedures, and safeguards. The Accountability Mechanism reinforces the rule of law by providing a framework that affected persons could resort to for the protection of their rights in case their grievances remain unresolved after going through the project grievance redress mechanisms and complaints resolution at the operations department level.

Related Lessons

The rule of law requires impartial and due application of legal frameworks, which in the ADB context requires adherence to its policies, procedures, and safeguards. For instance, appropriate environmental categorization for sensitive projects is crucial to ensure that appropriate safeguards and mitigation measures will be in place (e.g., Georgia Sustainable Urban Transport Project).

Adherence to the requirements of a comprehensive assessment of baseline conditions is critical because such studies inform project planning and the design and monitoring of effective mitigation measures (e.g., India Mundra Power Project).

ADB must exert efforts to continuously improve executing and implementing agency understanding of ADB safeguard policies. An adequate understanding of such policies is indispensable for their proper enforcement during project implementation (e.g., India Mundra Power Project).

---

[17] Footnote 8.

Timely identification of gaps between ADB policies and a national legal framework is essential (e.g., Indonesia Citarum Water Project). This example stems from a case handled under the 2003 Accountability Mechanism Policy (AMP), but the lesson continues to be relevant.

Compliance review contributes to the rule of law by being a catalyst for reforms by both ADB and the government (e.g., Sri Lanka Transport Development Project; CAREC Transport Project both under the 2003 AMP).

Reforms geared toward the rule of law—such as institutional innovation and improvements based on the national policy, legal, and political context—can contribute to the speedy and effective handling of complaints and prevent recourse to the judicial system by affected persons (e.g., Viet Nam CMDRCP).

Standard procedures and prescribed timelines for purposes of the GRM will help prevent impressions of inaction or sentiments that the concerns of affected persons are not being considered adequately. For this purpose, improved structures for the GRM with procedures, timelines, the composition of the Grievance Redress Committee, and clear roles and responsibilities of the GRM members are invaluable (e.g., Georgia Sustainable Urban Transport Project, Mongolia Ulaanbaatar GADIP).

RESPONSIVENESS

Good governance requires that institutions and processes try to serve all stakeholders within a reasonable time frame, in a manner adapted to the legitimate expectations and needs of the stakeholders.[18]

The Accountability Mechanism paves the way for development projects to become more responsive to the needs of stakeholders and/or affected persons both through problem-solving and compliance review functions, whereby appropriate remedies are rendered within specific time frames.

Related Lessons

Responsiveness requires ADB to ensure that adequate basic services for affected persons in cases of resettlement—such as water and electricity supply, nearby schools and medical facilities, debt work out, or income restoration programs—are made available, if appropriate. An analysis of the alternatives for resettlement, compensation, and livelihood restoration would further help prevent the impoverishment of the affected persons and provide ample opportunities to improve their livelihood (e.g., Cambodia Railway Project and Indonesia Citarum Water Project both under the 2003 AMP).

The Accountability Mechanism process may facilitate prompt action by the implementing agency and other concerned parties, thereby increasing the responsiveness of the project to stakeholders (e.g., Georgia Batumi Bypass Road Project, Mongolia Ulaanbaatar GADIP).

---

[18]   Footnote 8; Council of Europe. 2022. *12 Principles of Good Governance*.

Responsiveness in the form of a crafted remedial action plan informed by studies completed on schedule and focused on practical solutions to address harm is paramount to affected persons (e.g., Georgia Sustainable Urban Transport Project).

Responsiveness to stakeholders may also come in the form of adapting the project GRM to the local context and designing the same under national and local legislation and online systems (e.g., Mongolia Ulaanbaatar GADIP).

Responsiveness entails assisting the affected persons in both the process of displacement and the grievance resolution process. Otherwise, grievances may be escalated to the courts rather than the GRM because the affected persons did not have the capacity and knowledge to resort to the GRM (e.g., Sri Lanka Clean Energy Project).

EQUITY AND INCLUSIVENESS

A society's well-being—which can be seen as a consequence of good governance—depends on ensuring that all its members feel that they have a stake in it and do not feel excluded from mainstream society.[19] Such inclusiveness requires that all groups—particularly the most vulnerable—have opportunities to improve or maintain their well-being.[20]

Equity and inclusiveness—when the concerns of the most vulnerable people are addressed—are a direct effect of problem solving and remedial action, both functions of the offices of the Accountability Mechanism.

Related Lessons

The accurate identification of the affected persons and an inclusive and comprehensive consultation process are essential for good governance. Inadequate identification of—and consultation with—affected persons will likely result in gaps in the implementation of mitigation measures (e.g., India Mundra Power Project; Georgia Sustainable Urban Transport Project).

Through compliance review, recommendations for increased attention to project gender concerns improve inclusivity. This is illustrated in the 2003 AMP case of the Sri Lanka Southern Transport Development Project where an underpass designed with insufficient lighting increased risks to women disproportionately, adversely affecting them.

Remedial actions may come in the form of conducting inclusive, adequate, need-based, and transparent stakeholder consultations to establish and address the impact of the project on the livelihood of the different groups of affected persons, essentially addressing the issue of inclusiveness in the project. (e.g., India Mundra Power Project, Georgia Sustainable Urban Transport Project).

---

[19]   Footnote 8.
[20]   Footnote 8.

EFFECTIVENESS AND EFFICIENCY

Good governance means that processes and institutions produce results that meet the needs of society while making the best use of resources at their disposal. The concept of efficiency in the context of good governance can also be viewed through an environmental lens, also covering the sustainable use of natural resources and the protection of the environment.[21]

Effectiveness and efficiency are fostered by the Accountability Mechanism, which increases efficiency in terms of costs, compliance, and processes, generally enhancing development effectiveness.

Related Lessons

ADB should address inadequate reviews of impact assessments due to a lack of technical expertise, to ensure environmental protection (e.g., India Mundra Power Project, Georgia Sustainable Urban Transport Project). ADB should diligently assess project impacts to provide effective and timely assistance to project implementers where needed and to ensure adherence to the ADB Safeguard Policy Statement (SPS).

Adequate allocation of resources commensurate to the specific needs of a project is critical to achieving efficiency. For instance, ADB should obtain high-quality and credible valuation of properties for projects with significant land acquisition such as roads and highways, even if this means costlier valuation services (e.g., Georgia Batumi Bypass Road Project).

Compliance review may enhance the effective implementation of involuntary resettlement safeguards through institutional and systemic reforms, improving the effectiveness of future similar projects (e.g., the Sri Lanka Transport Development Project under the 2003 AMP). It may also reveal deficiencies in baseline studies on environmental conditions (e.g., pollution) and pave the way for an improvement in air quality and emissions modeling (e.g., Philippines Visayas Power Project under the 2003 AMP).

The efficiency of a project could be improved if each level of the GRM has the authority to decide on the complaints and grievances, shortening the turnaround time for solving them. An effective GRM significantly contributes to the timeliness in addressing the grievances and complaints at the project level and preventing their escalation. This also results in a cost-effective, accessible, and credible problem-solving process (e.g., Sri Lanka iRoad Program).

Periodic capacity building and training for various GRM actors, project staff, and consultants on communication and soft skills could improve communication with affected persons and complaint handling, improving project effectiveness and efficiency (e.g., Mongolia Ulaanbaatar GADIP). The allocation of the necessary human, technical, and financial resources to support project implementation and supervision is also necessary for grievance management and complaint handling (e.g., Mongolia Ulaanbaatar GADIP).

---

[21]   Footnote 8.

ACCOUNTABILITY

Accountability is a key requirement of good governance. Government institutions—as well as the private sector and civil society organizations—must be accountable to the public and their institutional stakeholders. In general, an organization or an institution is accountable to those who will be affected by its decisions or actions.[22] Accountability can be said to be the essence of the Accountability Mechanism, which enforces the accountability of ADB to affected persons.

Related Lessons

ADB is ultimately accountable for the impact of a project under the Accountability Mechanism and must be aware of design changes and any instances of noncompliance with its policies. The ADB project team must promptly track changes in project design and implementation to avoid harmful impacts (e.g., India Mundra Power Project). Site visits and project monitoring are essential for this (e.g., Mongolia Ulaanbaatar GADIP, CAREC Transport Project under the 2003 AMP).

Accountability may be exercised through prompt assessment and corrective actions to mitigate harm and reduce additional project costs (e.g., lessons learned from the India Mundra Power Project).

In cases of improper valuation of property acquired for development projects, additional measures for penalizing or fining non-compliant valuators could strengthen policies and reinforce accountability and good governance (e.g., Georgia Sustainable Urban Transport Project). This practice could also be considered for other instances of noncompliance.

Accountability Mechanism procedures may bring about the functioning improvement of the GRM through recommendations and the capacity building of implementing agencies as part of the complaints handling process, aiding accountability (e.g., Viet Nam CMDRCP, Mongolia Ulaanbaatar GADIP).

---

[22] Footnote 8.

The coal-fired power plant constructed under the Philippines Visayas Base-Load Power Development Project. The plant uses circulating fluidized bed (CFB) boiler technology, known as "cleaner coal" technology because it generates very low nitrogen oxide and sulfur dioxide emissions (photo by ADB).

Recurring and Emerging Issues in Independent Accountability Mechanisms and ADB That May Impact Good Governance

Several issues have emerged in the Accountability Mechanism domain, including reprisal or retaliation risk, the availability of effective remedies, allegations of human rights violations, and the efficiency of tracking complaints. This joint learning report inquires into these issues which may have a two-way interaction with the mechanism.

Participation in the Accountability Mechanism processes may be hampered and disincentivized due to the impact of these issues. For instance, complainants may not file complaints due to fear of reprisal. Human rights issues may create a similar fear. Ineffective remedies or delayed action on complaints may give rise to doubts about whether resorting to the Accountability Mechanism is worthwhile. Reduced participation and support for the mechanism may compromise good governance in the long run.

On the other hand, a robust accountability mechanism and good governance will help minimize—if not resolve—these issues. The participatory nature of good governance, for example, can pave the way for a good relationship between ADB and government agencies that may help safeguard reprisal or human rights concerns.

Considering the interaction of these issues with the Accountability Mechanism, ADB must adequately consider their significance to good governance.

Issue 1: Retaliation and/or Reprisal Risk—An Issue of Accountability and Rule of Law

The term "retaliation" or "reprisal" refers to any detrimental act—whether direct or indirect—that is advocated, threatened, or taken against a person involved or planning to be involved in an accountability mechanism process, and that is justifiably understood to be associated with that involvement.[23] Such detrimental acts may include harassment, threats, violence, damage to property, discriminatory treatment, impairment or harm, or threats to impair or harm the person, directly or indirectly, or the person's property, and the withholding of entitlements.[24]

The risk of retaliation and reprisal has become a growing concern in the accountability mechanism work of international financial institutions (IFIs), prompting discussions across Independent Accountability Mechanisms (IAM: i.e., the IAM Network, a network of 21 IFI IAMs).

---

[23] ADB. 2018. *Guidelines for the Protection of Key Stakeholders During the Accountability Mechanism Process.* Manila.
[24] Footnote 23.

If unresolved, reprisal risk can seriously hinder accountability mechanism processes and undermine good governance. Reprisal risk may specifically inhibit accountability when project-affected people refrain from filing meritorious complaints. Reprisal risk also impairs equity and inclusiveness, excluding underprivileged complainants from avenues for protecting their rights. The impact of possible reprisal is amplified in an accountability mechanism, as complainants are generally socioeconomically disadvantaged or underprivileged.

In response, international organizations—including IFIs—have formulated responses, measures, and tools to address this serious risk. Several members of the IAM Network have developed internal guidelines on reprisal and/or retaliation. [25]

ADB Experience and Response: Case Examples and Policies on Reprisals

Compliance Review Cases

In the case of ADB, one of the earliest instances (before the 2012 Accountability Mechanism Policy) that the risk of reprisal was broached was in a transport-related project, where the complainants alleged loss of homes, loss of livelihood, damage to the environment, dispersion of integrated communities, damage to temples, and "harsh and inhumane" resettlement practices. Three complainants—represented by a civil society group—requested that their names be kept confidential, specifically to protect them from threats and intimidations, as well as pressures that have arisen and probably will arise from this project.

Similar requests for confidentiality of the identities of the complainants were made in the complaints for a compliance review in several transport projects and a power project. In one transport project—in addition to the complainants—the nongovernment organization (NGO) that supported the complaint also asked not to be publicly named. While the complaints did not explicitly mention the risk of reprisal, it can be reasonably inferred that their requests for confidentiality were motivated by similar risks or concerns. In a more specific instance of possible reprisal, the complainant even withdrew a complaint due to the risk of retaliation and harassment of a relative who was a personnel of a project implementing agency. In another instance, the complaint led to a change from compliance review to problem solving.

Another request for confidentiality of the complainants' identities was made in a housing project. The complainants shared specific instances of harassment with the Accountability Mechanism. To address the risk of reprisal in this instance, the CRP took actions to ensure confidentiality in connection with various disclosure requirements:[26]

(i)   OCRP published only that a complaint was received without disclosing the contents or subject matter of the complaint itself. This is consistent with the Accountability Mechanism Policy, Appendix 9, para. 3 (i) and (ii), which requires the disclosure of the complaint letter (or request for compliance review), or in lieu thereof, a general description of the complaint if the complainant does not consent to the disclosure.

[25]   For instance, the World Bank identified certain preventive measures in response to the risk of retaliation: World Bank. 2018. *Guidelines to Reduce Retaliation Risks and Respond to Retaliation During the Panel Process.* Washington, DC. pp. 2–4. Similarly, the Inter-American Development Bank, developed a guide: T. Holstrom. 2019. *Guide for Independent Accountability Mechanisms on Measures to Address the Risk of Reprisals in Complaint Management.* Washington, DC: Inter-American Development Bank.
[26]   ADB. 2022. Addressing the Threat of Reprisal. Report by Irum Ahsan, Advisor, Office of the Compliance Review Panel. Manila.

(ii)   Since disclosure of the eligibility report together with management's response are both required, the eligibility report was sensitively drafted and disclosed and the management response redacted, and were shared only with the Board with no internal or public disclosure.

(iii)   When the complaint was forwarded to the operations department due to ineligibility for lack of prior good faith efforts to resolve the issues with the department, the CRP withheld documents that could disclose the identities of the complainants, providing them with department contact details and leaving it to their discretion whether to take it up with them.

(iv)   During the Board Compliance Review Committee meeting to discuss the eligibility report which—as a practice—is attended by other Board members and/or their advisors, the meeting was restricted only to the committee members and their legal advisor from the Office of the General Counsel.

(v)   The CRP ensured that e-systems only allowed Board members access to the eligibility report and included a special disclosure note highlighting that the report falls under exceptions to disclosure following special protocols.

All these were done under item B. Exceptions to Disclosure, para. 16 of the Access to Information Policy, which allows a certain exception to disclosure based on ADB's determination that disclosure of certain types of information may lead to harm outweighing the benefits of disclosure.

Problem-Solving Cases

In an urban infrastructure project, the OSPF received a complaint on the potential impacts of the project, especially related to the open blasting techniques in excavating streets for laying sewer lines. The complainants requested their identities be kept confidential due to the fear of being targeted by government agencies since they raised an earlier complaint with their municipality. The sensitivities associated with the disclosure of information related to the complaint were addressed identically to the process detailed in items (i) to (iii) of the preceding paragraph. As part of the eligibility determination for the complaint, OSPF carried out extensive discussions with the ADB project team on the need to protect the identities of the complainants while working effectively to resolve the complaints. It was agreed that there would be a single focal point from ADB who would communicate with the complainants and relay the concerns of the complainants to the implementing agency. The ADB project team worked with the executing agency and successfully addressed issues in the complaint while maintaining confidentiality.

The issue resurfaced in the project in a 2022 complaint by the same complainants for the restoration of damaged roads after the completion of sewer laying works. Requesting to keep their identities confidential, the complainants raised concerns that the internal road in front of their residence was not restored after the completion of sewer laying works. The complainants were of the view that the failure or refusal to restore was due to the earlier complaint that was submitted to ADB regarding controlled blasting adopted for excavating streets for laying sewer lines. OSPF worked closely with the project team to have the issues addressed and ensure that the road restoration activities were taken up promptly. The complainants eventually withdrew the complaint after written representation from the implementing agency on the implementation of the road restoration activities. Throughout the process, the ADB project team ensured the confidentiality of the identities of the complainants and ensured protection from any retaliation risks.

In a road and urban services project, two NGOs representing complainants submitted a third complaint. The affected persons were part of earlier complaints due to the loss of their residential land. ADB initiated a re-measurement of the complainants' property, despite agreement on previous property measurements and compensation. The complainants perceived that the remeasurement process that delayed the receipt of compensation was a form of harassment. The NGOs alleged that the complainants were potentially being singled out because they were the representatives in the complaint. The OSPF—through its national facilitator—provided support to the complainants to ensure that their compensation was received, and any further delays avoided. The OSPF national facilitator discussed the issue of retaliation with national and local officials responsible for the overall implementation of the ADB-supported project. Joint meetings with the offices of the local land management office and municipality ensured that the gaps in documentation were effectively addressed and the compensation payments given were consistent with the ordinance issued by the municipality.

In another ADB-assisted project, complainants refused to attend meetings with the OSPF after a government "notice" warned against negative comments targeting projects implemented with foreign aid. According to the "notice," such activities would be monitored, analyzed, and acted upon following prevailing laws. The complainants requested that their identities be kept confidential for their safety and that of their families, and discontinued communication. OSPF recommended the publication of a press release stating that the GRM and Accountability Mechanism processes remained accessible to all project-affected people. This illustrates how any threat of retaliatory action against the complainant—whether intentional or not—can create a "prior restraint" and "chilling effect" that may deter the filing of complaints.

ADB Policies Pertinent to the Risk of Reprisal

ADB protects against the risk of reprisals or retaliation for its staff through a comprehensive Code of Conduct and Whistleblower and Witness Protection.[27] However, ADB does not have an institutional statement on zero tolerance for reprisal against project-affected people or civil society organizations that may raise a complaint against an ADB-funded project. The ADB Accountability Mechanism offices are guided by the AMP, read with the Access to Information Policy while dealing with instances of retaliation in projects. For further guidance, the Guidelines for the Protection of Key Stakeholders during the Accountability Mechanism Process were developed, which are used internally by the mechanism offices.[28]

The AMP provides for the confidentiality of the identities of complainants, which will help protect parties from the risk of reprisal. It also allows the CRP to take necessary steps to ensure confidentiality. The complaint receiving officer is also directed to take necessary measures to ensure the confidentiality of complainants' identities. The policy also provides some guidance on maintaining an "appropriate degree of confidentiality" during problem solving and compliance review.

The ADB Access to Information Policy allows information not to be disclosed when disclosure would likely endanger the life, health, safety, or security of any individual, ADB assets, or the national security of a member.[29]

---

[27] ADB. 2012. ADB Code of Conduct (Administrative Order No. 2.02). Manila; ADB. 2017. Whistleblower and Witness Protection (Administrative Order No. 2.10). Manila.

[28] ADB. Guidelines for the Protection of Key Stakeholders during the Accountability Mechanism Process. Manila.

[29] ADB. 2018. ADB Access to Information Policy. Manila.

To address the risk of reprisal in the Accountability Mechanism process, ADB issued guidelines that are intended to address the security concerns raised during the process by affected persons made vulnerable by their generally underprivileged socioeconomic status.[30] It also provides that the risk of retaliation and its likely severity will be assessed early and throughout the Accountability Mechanism process and provides for precautionary procedures to be followed.[31]

Despite these processes, reprisals are a growing concern especially when Accountability Mechanism offices send the complainants back to the operations departments to exert good faith efforts to resolve the issues as per the requirement of the AMP. In such cases, dealing with the risk of retaliation is beyond the control of the offices. This report provides some recommendations for the protection of affected communities against the risk of reprisals.

Issue 2: The Right to an Effective Remedy in the Accountability Mechanism—Concerning Accountability and Responsiveness

The Right to an Effective Remedy

Financial institutions play an important role in realizing sustainable development, especially in developing countries. However, some development projects result in adverse impacts due to their massive scale and the stakeholders involved. The right to an effective remedy for possible adverse impacts is becoming a pressing issue in development finance.

Remedying harms has been defined in literature as "restoring the situation of aggrieved persons to at least the situation that they would have been in had the harms not occurred."[32] Available remedies have been identified including (i) restitution, which seeks to restore the victims to their original situation before a human rights violation or harm occurred; (ii) compensation—or monetary reparation—which is usually resorted to when restitution is not possible; (iii) rehabilitation, which may include medical and psychological care and legal and social services; (iv) satisfaction, which is a broad category encompassing measures, often aiming to emphasize the wrongful nature of the harm, publicly and symbolically acknowledge suffering, and respect the dignity of those who have been harmed; and (v) guarantees of non-repetition, which aim to prevent the recurrence of similar harm in the future.[33]

Challenges to the Right to an Effective Remedy

With the possible negative impacts of development projects and the need for an effective remedy, the question of remedy can be undermined by conceptual confusion, mixed incentives, and unwarranted assumptions concerning the potential legal and financial exposure of development finance institutions.[34] A negative perception of the remedy (e.g., finger-pointing, blame-shifting,

[30] Footnote 29, para. 5.
[31] Footnote 29.
[32] United Nations Human Rights, Office of the High Commissioner. 2022. *Remedy and Development Finance: Guidance and Practice*. New York and Geneva.
[33] Center for International Environmental Law. 2022. *Remedying Harm: Lessons from International Law for Development Finance* citing K. Schmalenbach. 2017. Max Planck Encyclopedia of Public International Law, International Organizations or Institutions, Legal Remedies against Acts of Organs. pp. 7–9.
[34] United Nations Human Rights, Office of the High Commissioner. 2022. *Remedy and Development Finance: Guidance and Practice*. New York and Geneva.

and risk aversion) can stigmatize the issue and discourage innovation and contingency planning. There may also be a tendency to focus on the financial costs of the remedy, disregarding its developmental benefits and the costs of failing to address them.[35] As a result, there may be a disconnect between the responsibility for providing a remedy and the readiness to provide it.

In the face of such concerns, effective remedies may become inaccessible to people affected by development projects. Development institutions must address the issue of remedy so that real and effectual redress can be given to project-affected people without compromising their systems and resources, which weakens development objectives. Access to an effective remedy for affected persons directly bolsters the responsiveness and accountability of the institutions concerned, as well as the effectiveness and efficiency of their development projects, aiding good governance.

ADB Response to the Right to an Effective Remedy in the Accountability Mechanism

ADB adopts a set of specific safeguard requirements that borrowers and/or clients are required to meet addressing environmental and social impacts and risks to help borrowers and/or clients and their projects achieve desired outcomes.[36] ADB will not finance projects that do not comply with its Safeguard Policy Statement (SPS), nor will it finance projects that do not comply with a host country's social and environmental laws and regulations, including those laws implementing host country obligations under international law.[37]

A project team is mandated to ensure that legal agreements include adequate covenants to address the implementation of the SPS.[38] If any of the safeguard requirements that are covenanted in the legal agreements are not satisfactorily met, ADB requires the borrower and/or client to develop and implement an agreed upon corrective action plan. ADB may also consider exercising its specified legal remedies, including suspension, cancellation, or acceleration of maturity.[39] Safeguards violations may be remedied by requiring a halt to civil works, a delay in disbursements, changes in project scope, additional finance, or enhanced monitoring and oversight.[40]

At or beyond project closure, remedies may come in the form of audits of outstanding issues and corrective action; project extensions to complete corrective actions; use of escrow accounts for compensation; corrective actions linked to a new loan or tranche; and government finance or commitment on further actions.[41] More drastic options such as loan suspension, advancing of maturity, and cancellation are available but seldom used.

The ADB Accountability Mechanism Policy mandates that management propose remedial actions to bring a project causing harm into compliance after board approval.[42] Remedial action may also be

---

[35]   Footnote 34.
[36]   ADB. Operations Manual F1/BP- SPS, para. 5.
[37]   ADB. Operations Manual F1/BP- SPS, para. 6.
[38]   ADB. Operations Manual F1/OP- SPS, para. 24.
[39]   ADB. Operations Manual F1/OP- SPS, para. 28; ADB. Operations Manual J4/BP, para. 6; PAI 5.08. Project Performance Monitoring. para. 17; Ordinary Operations. Concessional Loan Regulations, Section 8.01(c), 8.02 (a), 8.07.
[40]   ADB. 2022. Implementing Remedy under Changing Circumstance. Presentation to the Board Compliance Review Committee by the Sustainable Development and Climate Change Department (now Climate Change and Sustainable Development Department). 10 March.
[41]   Footnote 40.
[42]   ADB. 2012. *Accountability Mechanism Policy 2012.*

adopted because of the Accountability Mechanism problem-solving process.[43] Remedies previously delivered have included

- (i)   compensation deficit payment schemes due to undervaluation of land and other assets acquired from affected persons,
- (ii)   improved facilities on resettlement sites with inadequate basic services,
- (iii) improved functioning of the grievance redress mechanism,
- (iv)   debt workout scheme to address indebtedness and impoverishment due to inadequate compensation and loss of income following involuntary resettlement,
- (v)   income and/or livelihood restoration plans following involuntary resettlement,
- (vi)   requirement of full compensation payment before actual resettlement,
- (vii) provision of complete project information to each affected household,
- (viii) detailed project framework for benefit monitoring and evaluation activities,
- (ix)   continuous air quality monitoring following failure to address ambient air quality monitoring requirements,
- (x)   gap analysis comparing national laws with ADB SPS following noncompliance due to difficulties in handling the distinctions between the two frameworks,
- (xi)   staff resourcing to address resettlement issues as early as possible,
- (xii) additional technical assistance, and
- (xiii) medical assistance for affected persons whose health was adversely affected by the project.

Effective remedies require financial resources. Funding such resources can become a dilemma when the remedy (such as a corrective action plan) is proposed by ADB and implemented by the borrower. This is even more difficult in the case of public financing where government accountability and financial liability are complex. Government procedures for appropriation and public use of funds must be complied with while issues of immunity could be raised. Private sector borrowers could pretermimate (pay off) a project loan when remedies have not been fully implemented to avoid having to deal with a complaint.

Effective but sustainable remedies necessitate a high degree of creativity. An appropriate or effective remedy is not limited to any single form, and can be more expansive and combine several forms of remedies or integrate remedies with reforms. System improvements and reforms—which will address the root of the harm or prevent it—may be more effective and realistic than isolated instances of redress. For instance, improvements to stakeholder engagement and grievance redress mechanisms that address concerns promptly may simplify and minimize the extent—and expense—of remedies required.

Issue 3: Human Rights Concerns

Accountability Mechanism complaints have raised the subject of human rights violations, particularly referring to the right to be protected from forced eviction; the right to adequate housing after physical relocation; the right to an affordable and adequate supply of water in relocation sites; the right to be free from discrimination on the grounds of property and land tenure status; the right of every child to an adequate standard of living for the child's physical, mental, spiritual, moral, and social development; the right of every child to the enjoyment of the highest attainable standard of

---

[43]   Footnote 42, para. 171.

health; the right of every child affected by the project to education based on equal opportunity; and the right to an effective remedy for persons whose rights have been violated.[44]

A review of ADB corporate, environmental, and social policies and strategies confirms that human rights considerations are embedded across such policies and strategies.

ADB Strategy 2030 contains several operational priorities that can bolster human rights including addressing remaining poverty and reducing inequalities, accelerating progress in gender equality, and creating an enabling environment for sustainable growth.

The ADB SPS aims to avoid, minimize, mitigate, and/or compensate for adverse impacts of projects, effectively protecting the rights of affected persons in three key safeguard areas.[45]

   (i)   **The Environmental Safeguards** are aimed at risks to physical, biological, socioeconomic (including impacts on livelihood through environmental media, health and safety, vulnerable groups, and gender issues), and physical cultural resources.
   (ii)   **The Involuntary Settlements Safeguards** are aimed at the adverse impacts of involuntary resettlements, protecting the livelihood and standards of living of the displaced and vulnerable groups.
   (iii) **The Indigenous Peoples Safeguards** foster full respect for indigenous peoples' identity, dignity, human rights, livelihood systems, and cultural uniqueness as defined by the indigenous peoples themselves.

The policy statement for each of the three safeguard areas mandate meaningful consultation with the affected persons and other stakeholders. Moreover, the SPS has an ADB Prohibited Investment Activities List containing activities that do not qualify for ADB financing including production or activities involving harmful or exploitative forms of forced labor or child labor, and production of or trade in any product or activity deemed illegal under host country laws or regulations or international conventions and agreements or subject to international phaseouts or bans, among others. The SPS is being updated as of 2023.

The ADB Social Protection Strategy promotes good social protection practices in line with core labor standards: (i) freedom of association and the effective recognition of the right to collective bargaining; (ii) elimination of all forms of forced or compulsory labor; (iii) effective abolition of child labor; and (iv) elimination of discrimination in respect of employment and occupation.[46]

The ADB Gender and Development Policy has key elements that include gender sensitivity, gender analysis, gender planning, mainstreaming, and agenda setting.[47] The policy directly addresses gender disparities by designing a larger number of projects with gender and development either as a primary or secondary objective.

The ADB Access to Information Policy has an overarching principle of clear, timely, and appropriate disclosure, and favors proactive disclosure and information sharing that is timely enough to allow

---

[44] For example, the Cambodia Railway Project, and Sri Lanka Southern Transport Development Project, although filed prior to the 2012 Accountability Mechanism where the complaints explicitly referred to alleged "human rights violations."
[45] ADB. 2009. *Safeguard Policy Statement*. Manila.
[46] ADB. 2001. *Social Protection Strategy*. Manila.
[47] ADB. 1998. *Gender and Development Policy*. Manila.

stakeholders to provide meaningful inputs and feedback.[48] There are also limited exceptions to full disclosure of information, considering the need to protect a personnel's right to privacy and certain client information.

ADB borrowers and clients must legally comply with ADB environmental and social policies, and the environmental and social legal framework of the project's host country. This allows ADB to take legal actions such as suspension, cancellation, or acceleration of the maturity of the related grant or loan in the event of non-compliance.

The ADB Accountability Mechanism Policy embeds human rights considerations through its compliance review function. The function investigates alleged ADB noncompliance with its operational policies and procedures that has caused—or is likely to cause—direct and material harm to project-affected people. The problem-solving function responds to the problems of local people affected by ADB-assisted projects through a range of informal and flexible methods.[49]

Issue 4: The Need for Effective Complaint Handling and Tracking by Operations Departments—A Matter of Transparency, Responsiveness, and Accountability

The effective handling and tracking of complaints are key to good governance since ineffective handling and tracking impair transparency, responsiveness, and accountability. The ability to monitor the progress of a complaint and provide information on ongoing proceedings is essential to a transparent process. Responsiveness to a complaint or project also depends on the availability of information via effective complaints tracking.

As part of project design and implementation, operations departments provide daily problem prevention, problem solving, and prevention of noncompliance with ADB operational policies and procedures. During the Accountability Mechanism processes, operations departments contribute to smooth problem-solving and provide necessary cooperation for effective compliance review. Operations departments are a key part of ensuring the implementation of remedial actions because of the mechanism processes.[50]

One of the roles of the operations departments is the handling of complaints that were filed to the Accountability Mechanism but found to be ineligible by the SPF or CRP for lack of prior good faith efforts by the complainants to solve the problems or issues with the relevant operations department.[51] Under the 2012 AMP, operations departments are mandated to address problems or issues relating to ineligible complaints forwarded to them by the SPF or CRP because the complainants did not make prior good-faith efforts to solve the problems or issues with the departments.[52] In addition to addressing problems or issues relating to ineligible complaints forwarded to them by the SPF or CRP because the complainants did not make prior good-faith efforts to solve the problems or issues with the departments, operations departments are specifically mandated in para. 195 of the AMP to track the process and results in resolving these

---

[48]   ADB. 2018. *Access to Information Policy*. Manila
[49]   ADB. 2012. *Accountability Mechanism Policy 2012*. Manila.
[50]   Footnote 49, para. 197.
[51]   Footnote 49, para. 164.
[52]   Footnote 49, paras. 195–197.

complaints. Operations departments can develop a tracking system or take advantage of the system developed by the OSPF in 2009.[53]

Cross-Section of the Complaints Handled by Operations Departments

This report examined complaints by 20 parties that were forwarded to different operations departments due to ineligibility under the Accountability Mechanism process for lack of prior good faith (Figure 7).

Figure 7: Years Pending with Operations Departments
(as of October 2022)

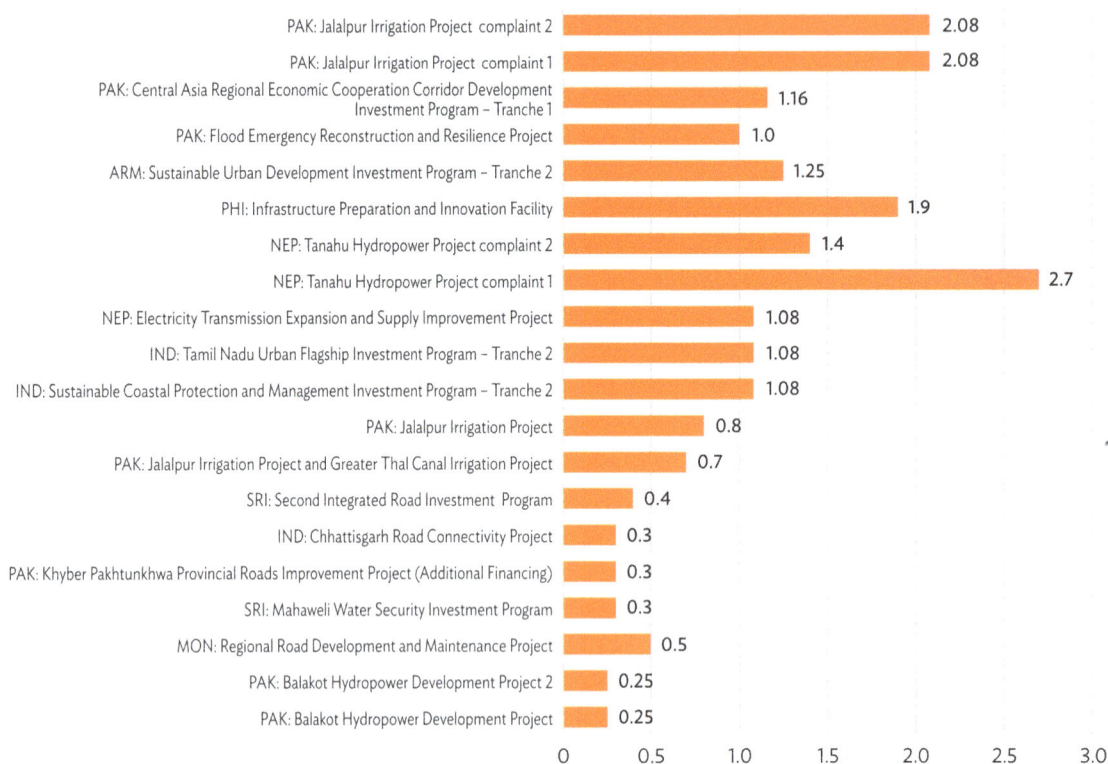

Project	Years
PAK: Jalalpur Irrigation Project complaint 2	2.08
PAK: Jalalpur Irrigation Project complaint 1	2.08
PAK: Central Asia Regional Economic Cooperation Corridor Development Investment Program – Tranche 1	1.16
PAK: Flood Emergency Reconstruction and Resilience Project	1.0
ARM: Sustainable Urban Development Investment Program – Tranche 2	1.25
PHI: Infrastructure Preparation and Innovation Facility	1.9
NEP: Tanahu Hydropower Project complaint 2	1.4
NEP: Tanahu Hydropower Project complaint 1	2.7
NEP: Electricity Transmission Expansion and Supply Improvement Project	1.08
IND: Tamil Nadu Urban Flagship Investment Program – Tranche 2	1.08
IND: Sustainable Coastal Protection and Management Investment Program – Tranche 2	1.08
PAK: Jalalpur Irrigation Project	0.8
PAK: Jalalpur Irrigation Project and Greater Thal Canal Irrigation Project	0.7
SRI: Second Integrated Road Investment Program	0.4
IND: Chhattisgarh Road Connectivity Project	0.3
PAK: Khyber Pakhtunkhwa Provincial Roads Improvement Project (Additional Financing)	0.3
SRI: Mahaweli Water Security Investment Program	0.3
MON: Regional Road Development and Maintenance Project	0.5
PAK: Balakot Hydropower Development Project 2	0.25
PAK: Balakot Hydropower Development Project	0.25

ARM = Armenia, IND = India , MON = Mongolia, NEP = Nepal, PAK = Pakistan, PHI = Philippines, SRI = Sri Lanka.

Source: Survey on complaints forwarded to the Operations Departments for lack of prior good faith efforts (OSPF Survey for Operations Departments), responses as of 15 September 2022.

---

[53] Footnote 49, para. 195.

Of 20 complaints forwarded to the operations departments from February 2020 to July 2022, 6 have been closed and 14 remain open as of 2023.

The reasons for complaint pendency include the ongoing implementation of the agreed course of action between the parties; a reshuffle of government ministers that delayed the process; the elevation of cases to a compensation review board pending approval of state government budget allocation; and pandemic travel restrictions causing meeting delays with community and/or NGO representatives, OSPF, and ADB project teams.

Pending case durations range from 3 months to 2.7 years (Figure 8).

Figure 8: Duration of Years Pending with Operations Departments (for Open Complaints)
(as of October 2022)

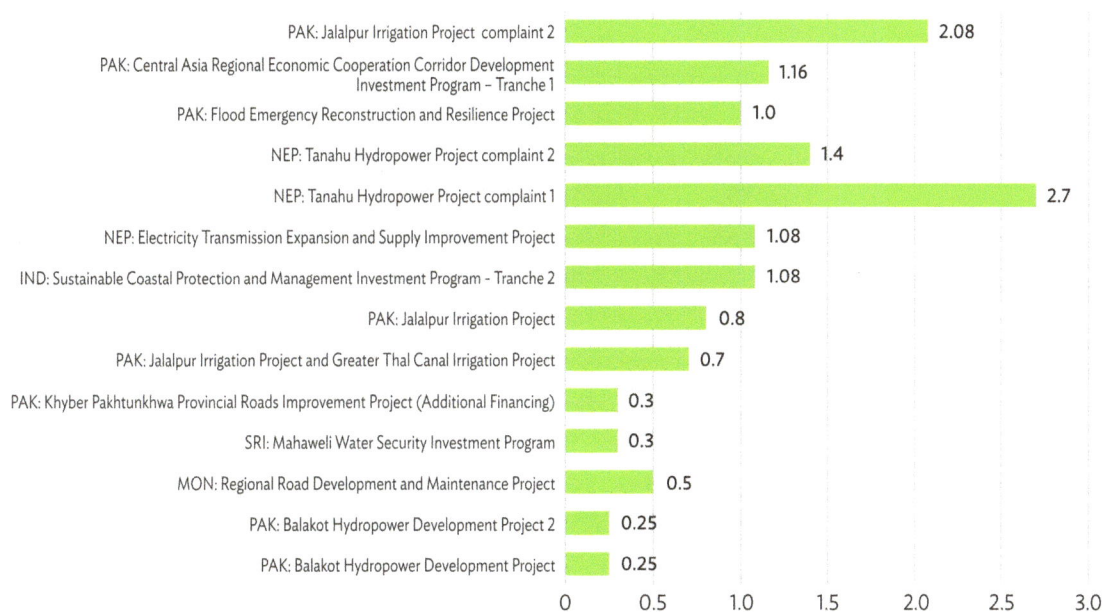

Project	Years
PAK: Jalalpur Irrigation Project complaint 2	2.08
PAK: Central Asia Regional Economic Cooperation Corridor Development Investment Program – Tranche 1	1.16
PAK: Flood Emergency Reconstruction and Resilience Project	1.0
NEP: Tanahu Hydropower Project complaint 2	1.4
NEP: Tanahu Hydropower Project complaint 1	2.7
NEP: Electricity Transmission Expansion and Supply Improvement Project	1.08
IND: Sustainable Coastal Protection and Management Investment Program - Tranche 2	1.08
PAK: Jalalpur Irrigation Project	0.8
PAK: Jalalpur Irrigation Project and Greater Thal Canal Irrigation Project	0.7
PAK: Khyber Pakhtunkhwa Provincial Roads Improvement Project (Additional Financing)	0.3
SRI: Mahaweli Water Security Investment Program	0.3
MON: Regional Road Development and Maintenance Project	0.5
PAK: Balakot Hydropower Development Project 2	0.25
PAK: Balakot Hydropower Development Project	0.25

IND = India , MON = Mongolia, NEP = Nepal, PAK = Pakistan, SRI = Sri Lanka.
Source: OSPF Survey for Operations Departments, responses as of 15 September 2022.

Among the complaints that have been closed, the time frame for their closure ranged from 4 months to 2.08 years (Figure 9).

Solutions for closed complaints included confirmation of measurements of structures for demolition, exclusion of a disputed road section from the contract due to failure to reach an amicable solution, and additional public consultations leading to the start of the project's civil works.[54]

Figure 9: Years to Closure (Closed Cases)

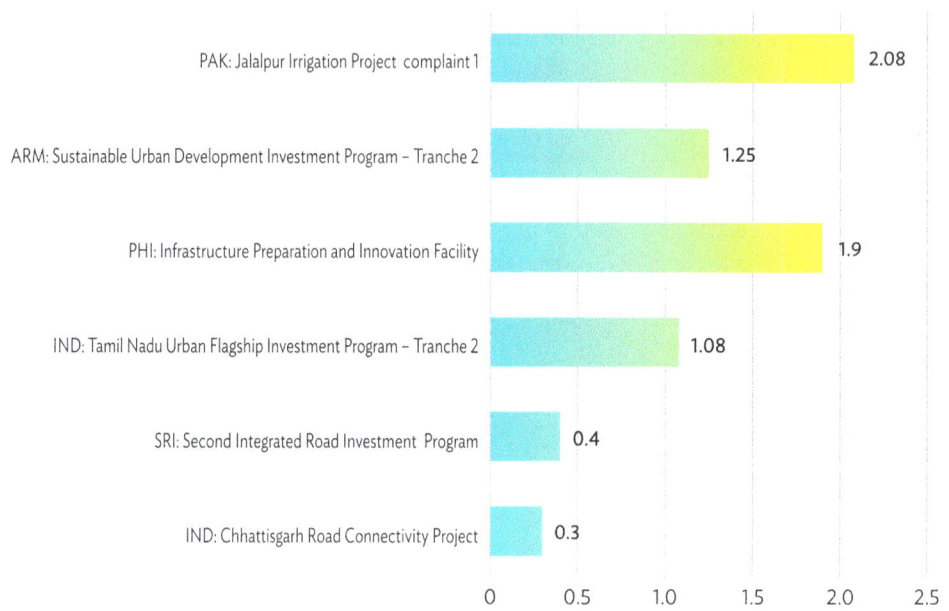

ARM = Armenia, IND = India , PAK = Pakistan, PHI = Philippines, SRI = Sri Lanka.
Source: OSPF Survey for Operations Departments, responses as of 15 September 2022.

---

[54] Survey on complaints forwarded to the Operations Departments for lack of prior good faith efforts (OSPF survey for operations departments), responses as of 15 September 2022.

Tracking of Complaints Handled by Operations Departments

Operations Departments Systems and Practices for Complaint Tracking

Operations departments have developed tracking systems for ineligible complaints that are forwarded to them, although they appear to use different complaint monitoring systems (Box 6). Most operations departments have developed tracking and monitoring systems for complaints received at the department or resident mission and for tracking ineligible complaints forwarded by the OCRP or OSPF.[55]

Box 6

Operations Departments Complaint Tracking Systems

The Southeast Asia Department (SERD) has a Safeguards Monitoring System based on the PowerApps platform for complaints and concerns received about the operations department or resident mission. For the tracking of complaints forwarded by the OSPF and OCRP, SERD generally makes use of the project complaint tracking (PCT) system established by OSPF, which links to the SERD Safeguards Monitoring System.

The East Asia Department (EARD) uses a safeguard monitoring database for tracking operations departments or resident mission complaints and concerns. The same system is used for tracking complaints forwarded by the OSPF and OCRP to the EAOD.

The Pacific Department (PARD) has a grievance resolution process for dealing with complaints or issues raised directly on PARD projects. For tracking complaints forwarded by the OSPF and OCRP, PARD has a grievance database initiated in April 2021 that records all project complaints (safeguard and non-safeguard) forwarded to it.

The South Asia Department (SARD) established the SARD Tracking System (STS) for tracking operations departments and resident mission complaints and grievances, as well as complaints received through the Accountability Mechanism and forwarded to SARD. This is a web-based platform for monitoring compliance with social and environmental safeguards and includes tracking each project with complaints received.

The Central and West Asia Department (CWRD) uses the project complaint tracking (PCT) system established by OSPF. PCT will also be linked to the CWRD Safeguards Monitoring system being developed. To complement the PCT, CWRD also uses an Excel-based monitoring sheet that is regularly forwarded to project teams to report on the status of problem-solving efforts for Accountability Mechanism-forwarded complaints.

The Private Sector Operations Department (PSOD) has a department-specific complaint-handling procedure that formally lists the required actions, timelines, and responsible parties, and integrates the tracker into the overall PSOD complaints-handling system. The system was launched in February 2022.

OCRP = Office of the Compliance Review Panel, OSPF = Office of the Special Project Facilitator.

Source: Survey on monitoring systems for operations departments-handled complaints (OCRP survey for operations departments), responses as of 15 September 2022.

---

[55] Survey on monitoring systems for Operations Departments-handled complaints (OCRP survey for operations departments), responses as of 15 September 2022.

Developing the Integrated Safeguards Management System

CCSD (formerly SDCC) is developing an IT solution called Integrated Safeguards Management System (ISMS)—for rollout and piloting by the end of 2023—to centrally manage all ADB environmental and social safeguards business processes. The ISMS will include an analytical module to generate diagnostic and analytical reports at both project and corporate levels, such as the annual Chief Compliance Officer's Report. The primary objective of the ISMS is to strengthen environmental and social safeguard implementation in ADB-supported projects by tracking and monitoring key environmental and social safeguard indicators at both the entry and exit of the ADB project cycle. The analytical and diagnostic functionalities within ISMS will facilitate early identification of key challenges with safeguards implementation—including identification of sector and/or regional trends—to enable the development of strategic and harmonized interventions to be addressed by the project, client and/or borrower, and/or ADB project teams.

The solution design of the ISMS has fully integrated with ADB IT-based systems for managing operations business processes—such as e-operations—and will be with future sovereign operations when completed. The procurement review system is also planned for integration when completed as a module within sovereign operations. The objective of these integrations is to minimize duplication of effort and optimize resource use efficiency by ensuring that all the systems have a single source of truth concerning project-related information to avoid multiple entries.

The ISMS is also integrated with the ADB Spatial Data Analysis Explorer to leverage its geospatial capabilities to strengthen safeguards implementation in ADB projects. To achieve this objective, the explorer has been enhanced as part of the ISMS solution design, with a toolkit to strengthen the environmental and social safeguards screening and categorization process. The screening toolkit aims to use environmental and social safeguards information prepared for selected approved ADB projects to enhance the screening and categorization process and upstream ADB due diligence to optimize project processing time and costs.

The solution design of ISMS includes the management of persistent project complaints and complaints directly lodged with ADB (via ADB headquarters and resident missions) to ensure they are adequately addressed. ISMS will integrate with the ADB Accountability Mechanism Complaints Tracking System to facilitate prompt communication between the two systems in responding to and tracking the management of complaints, especially for those deemed ineligible for the Accountability Mechanism. This integration and additional features within the ISMS will bolster good governance by ensuring confidentiality, promoting transparency, improving responsiveness, and optimizing efficient resource use.

Institutional Reforms and Recommendations

Based on the analysis of complaints triggers, lessons learned, and recurrent and emerging issues, several reforms and system improvements are required. Since the ADB SPS is undergoing an update, it is anticipated that a few, if not several issues, discussed in this report, may find resolution through the updated safeguards policy in the second half of 2023.

Ongoing Reform: Updating of the Safeguard Policy Statement

The Rationale for the Safeguard Policy Statement Update

The updating of the ADB SPS was initiated following an evaluation of the SPS by the Independent Evaluation Department (IED). The overall objective of the policy update is to strengthen safeguard implementation effectiveness and efficiency in ways that will enhance beneficial safeguards outcomes for the environment and affected persons.[56]

The ADB SPS update is a reform geared toward good governance since it is primarily directed at strengthening the effectiveness and efficiency of safeguard implementation to enhance beneficial safeguards outcomes and the responsiveness of ADB development projects.

The recommendations for the update are also oriented toward good governance. The IED evaluation recommended updating the ADB Safeguard Policy provisions and procedures, and more specifically that ADB

(i)   modernize the policy, increasing its relevance and customizing it for both sovereign and private sector financing, by building off ADB implementation experiences and recent updates at other multilateral financial institutions (MFIs), including customization to both public and private sector operations;

(ii)   adopt a new approach in the policy to strengthening borrower systems, with improvement and pragmatic use of country systems;

(iii)   introduce a new safeguards implementation framework including an updated oversight structure and reporting lines that are strengthened and contribute to more consistent safeguard outcomes across ADB;

(iv)   underpin the safeguards policy and implementation framework with sufficiently detailed policy guidance and a range of operational guidance documents and good practice notes with established mechanisms for regular review and updates; and

---

[56]   ADB. 2020. Background Information Paper for the Review and Update of the ADB Safeguards Policy Statement. Manila.

(v)   assess the necessary staffing complement to deliver the safeguards implementation framework and strengthen skills, empowering staff to deliver better safeguard outcomes.[57]

Increased relevance and customization (responsiveness), pragmatic use of country systems (effective and efficient), sufficiently detailed policy guidance (transparent), strengthening skills, and empowering staff (participatory) can all work toward good governance.

The IED review of the SPS concluded that the ADB approach to risk assessment—where risk and impact are incorrectly mixed in categorization—and management in the safeguards processes is inconsistent with the approach of comparator MFIs in 2022. There is an imbalance in the assessment and adaptive risk management between environmental and social issues, with relatively limited attention provided to social issues. Comparator MFIs are now considering social risks and impacts beyond resettlement and involvement of indigenous peoples. International good practice has also moved to integrated environmental and social categorization and assessment, and adaptive risk management during implementation.[58]

IED found that implementation outcomes for Indigenous Peoples Safeguards have been less than satisfactory as project activities in indigenous peoples-inhabited areas tend to be avoided. According to the IED report, the Indigenous Peoples Safeguards were not consistently triggered mainly because (i) indigenous peoples and/or ethnic minorities' impacts were often limited to involuntary resettlement, and (ii) many indigenous peoples or members of ethnic minorities were assumed with safeguard assessments to have already been mainstreamed into the economy in non-indigenous people majority areas. There is also a reluctance by some developing member countries (DMCs) to recognize and provide special entitlements to indigenous peoples' communities. Engagement with indigenous peoples' communities through the undertaking of social impact assessments was limited, which did not allow for adequate consultation and information disclosure.[59]

IED found that while the Involuntary Resettlement Safeguards performance is generally satisfactory, there is a predominant reliance on mitigation compensation of affected persons, and weaknesses in enhancing development outcomes in terms of livelihood restoration and improvement, and stakeholder consultation.[60]

The update is intended to enhance integration and synergy between environmental and social safeguards, address thematic crosscutting and emerging issues across environmental and social safeguards, and achieve better tailoring for new and existing lending instruments for sovereign and nonsovereign operations. IED recommended an institutional framework for enhanced safeguard oversight, staffing, and performance management.[61]

Status of the Policy Update

Following the IED recommendations, management tasked SDCC (now CCSD) to undertake a comprehensive review and update of the 2009 ADB SPS. The process has been undertaken in a consultative manner with the involvement of internal and external stakeholders, including DMCs,

---

[57]   ADB. 2020. Effectiveness of the 2009 Safeguard Policy Statement. Manila. p.1.
[58]   ADB. 2020. Effectiveness of the 2009 Safeguard Policy Statement. Manila. p. xii.
[59]   ADB. 2020. Effectiveness of the 2009 Safeguard Policy Statement. Manila. p. 42.
[60]   ADB. 2020. Effectiveness of the 2009 Safeguard Policy Statement. Manila. pp. 39–40.
[61]   Footnote 56, pp. 111–113.

civil society organizations, and project-affected persons. The revised safeguard policy is expected to be submitted to the ADB Board for consideration in the second half of 2023, with a subsequent rollout in 2023–2024 and effectivity in 2024.

Proposed Policy Architecture

The proposed policy is composed of (i) ADB Environmental and Social Policy covering overall objectives, policy principles, expected outcomes, risk categorization, due diligence, supervision, and implementation support; (ii) requirements for different financing modalities, and (iii) environmental and social policy standards (ESS) for borrowers and clients (Figure 10). To ensure better clarity and consistent implementation performance of the policy, DMC capacity will be improved and supported through a set of supporting tools and documents, including guidance notes for each of the ESSs, good practice notes, training and awareness material, sample terms of reference, and templates.

Figure 10: Environmental and Social Policy Standards

Environmental and Social Policy Standards (ESS)
Policy objectives, scope and requirements for borrowers and clients

1 ESS 1 Assessment and management of environment and social risks and impacts	**2 ESS 2** Labor and working conditions	**3 ESS 3** Pollution prevention and resource efficiency
4 ESS 4 Health, safety and security	**5 ESS 5** Land acquisition and involuntary resettlement	**6 ESS 6** Biodiversity and sustainable natural resource management	**10** Climate change
7 ESS 7 Indigenous people	**8 ESS 8** Cultural heritage	**9 ESS 9** Stakeholder engagement and information disclosure

Source: Sustainable Development and Climate Change Department (now Climate Change and Sustainable Development Department).

Safeguards Policy Updates and Their Impact on Good Governance

The 10 proposed ESSs may all contribute to good governance being directed toward strengthening the effectiveness and efficiency of safeguard implementation. However, the impact on good governance will most directly be seen under ESS 1 and ESS 9, which directly correspond to several characteristics of good governance. For instance, integrated safeguards monitoring under ESS 1 relates directly to responsiveness, while enhanced stakeholder engagement and information disclosure under ESS 9 will build on participation, consensus, and transparency.

Integrated Environment and Social Instruments

Newly proposed instruments under the updated SPS will make integrated safeguards management more adaptable and more responsive to the changing project environment. Proposed projects will require an Environmental and Social Impact Assessment, a stakeholder engagement plan that will cover both environmental and social safeguards, and an Environment and Social Commitment Plan, an agreement between ADB and the borrower that will set out measures and actions required for the project to meet the ESSs over a specified time frame, among others.

Improved Stakeholder Engagement and Grievance Mechanism

The proposed updated policy will have a separate ESS on stakeholder engagement and information disclosure. Provisions of the proposed ESS will enhance meaningful consultation and engagement throughout the project life cycle through more detailed provisions, more clarity and detailed guidance to the borrowers, and have verifiable indicators to monitor key stakeholder engagement and information disclosure processes. It will introduce a new safeguards instrument—the stakeholder engagement plan—which will be proportionate to the nature and scale of a project and its potential risks and impacts.

The SPS update also considers improvements to the design and functioning of the grievance mechanism through requirements to consider anonymous complaints; utilize traditional dispute resolution mechanisms; enable full and fair access by additional means for vulnerable and marginalized persons; and address allegations of retaliation, abuse, intimidation, or discrimination, if any. It considers special provisions on the monitoring and reporting and organizational capacity to support the proper functioning of the project GRM. For project workers or workers at risk of sexual exploitation, abuse, or harassment, separate grievance mechanisms will be established in addition to the grievance mechanism provided under ESS 9.

Future Reforms: Recommendations for Systemic Improvements

Based on the analysis of learning lessons and recurrent and emerging issues, this report presents the following recommendations for systemic improvements for enhanced accountability and good governance of ADB development work.

Recommendation 1: Robust Due Diligence

Many of the adverse impact triggers discussed in this report could be prevented or minimized through robust due diligence. Comprehensive and timely due diligence is instrumental in preventing direct and material harm or compliance issues. When these are avoided, minimized, and mitigated at the earliest possible stage, the cost of reparation and remedy goes down. Reputational risk can likewise be reduced. Although some improvements in this area may be captured in the updated SPS, the following recommendations are made for more robust due diligence:

(i)   Design Phase: *Due diligence standard and tailored criteria at the early stages of the project preparation.* Due diligence criteria must include both standardized and tailored components to capture risks that are common for the industry as well as risks that are unique to the project. Continuously upgraded and refined standardized due diligence criteria will capture the evolving nature of commonly encountered risks. A tailored component—designed to capture risks that may arise under the unique context and circumstances of the project, including cumulative impacts of the project and impacts on vulnerable communities—will ensure that a complete picture of the project risks is captured.

(ii)   **Implementation Phase:** *Predefined course of action beyond the determination of risks and issues during design due diligence.* Robust due diligence must have a predetermined course of action throughout project implementation to efficiently address risks and issues uncovered as part of project monitoring. This includes defined criteria on when to escalate the issues within ADB and with implementation partners to ensure timely compliance with policies, and for efficient mitigation of adverse project impacts. Otherwise, some risks might be left to those without the authority to address them.

Recommendation 2: Guidelines to Manage Adequate Human and Financial Resources for Safeguards Implementation

Procedural non-adherence triggers may arise due to inadequate resources and/or capacity. Responsiveness, accountability, and efficiency require adequate human and financial resources for efficient, safe, and compliant project implementation.

Proper financial and human resource management and planning may be instrumental in minimizing complaints triggered by a lack of transparency and meaningful consultation. Lack of adequate technical skills to conduct robust due diligence and inadequate human resources lead to a lack of participation and consensus.

Internal guidelines can be developed for enhanced management of human resources and financial governance in safeguards management.[62] This will enable effectiveness and efficiency as well as responsiveness in dealing with affected persons.

Recommendation 3: Institutional Response to Retaliation Risk

Retaliation or reprisals are a significant risk for ADB project stakeholders—especially for the most vulnerable people—and require an urgent response. While ADB provides a reasonable framework for the protection of its staff against retaliation risk, it also needs a robust framework to protect affected communities and civil society organizations against the risk of retaliation if they choose to bring a complaint against an ADB-funded project. The rationale is very strong that affected persons should not be further harmed by complaining to ADB.

As of 2023, only the Accountability Mechanism offices have adopted broad guidelines (Guidelines for the Protection of Key Stakeholders during the Accountability Mechanism Process) that provide some tools to be used when encountering risks of retaliation. However, these guidelines are outdated and are neither comprehensive nor accompanied by risk assessment tools, and are limited to the Accountability Mechanism offices. These guidelines—when used together with the relevant provisions of the AMP and Access to Information Policy—become useful tools.

ADB should state zero tolerance for retaliation against affected communities and civil society organizations for reinforcing accountability and the rule of law on protection and security for

---

[62] ADB. 2002. *Guidelines for the Financial Governance and Management of Investment Projects Financed by ADB.* Manila.

affected persons. ADB should also develop comprehensive guidelines and risk assessment tools for the mitigation of risks of retaliation in an efficient and timely manner.

The Accountability Mechanism offices should upgrade their guidelines and establish robust guidance toolkits to address this sensitive issue. This risk could be better managed through awareness-raising, training workshops, and initiatives. Initially, the Accountability Mechanism offices could partner with other departments like the Office of the Auditor General, the Office of Anticorruption and Integrity, the Office of Risk Management, and the Office of the Ombudsperson.

Since there is a need to rely on strong relations with governments to protect claimants from the risk of retaliation or reprisal, ADB should systematically engage with governments, where part of the regular agenda could be the discussion and monitoring of reprisal risk.

Systems for complaints tracking and monitoring can also incorporate elements to protect from this risk. For instance, the ISMS could incorporate indicators of retaliation risk among the key safeguard information that it will monitor.

Recommendation 4: Guidelines on the Escalation of Issues and Remedies

Remedies are complex without a single or straightforward measure for their resolution. Addressing issues around ineffective remedies—at best and realistically—requires the prevention or minimization of the harm. Systemic and institutional reforms to mitigate harm and adverse impacts promptly and under a system that is credible and trustworthy are needed.

ADB provides remedies at several points in a project, including problem solving or compliance reviews. The remedies at times are insufficient, either not commensurate with the adverse impact or due to significant delays. Appropriately identified remedies can get stuck at one level due to inaction and require prompt escalation of action from one authority to another within ADB. Harms can be left unresolved or aggravated without proper guidance on when to escalate an action to a certain authority or higher.

Internal operations level guidance on the escalation of issues and remedies would ensure that remedies are provided promptly. Some escalation indicators could be the length of time the issue is pending, the amount involved, the seriousness of the issue, the extent of impact if unresolved for an extended period, etc. These indicators can be incorporated into the centralized complaints tracking system.

Recommendation 5: Strengthening Project-Level Implementation of Safeguard Policy Statement for Human Rights Considerations

Analysis has concluded that ADB policies and strategies reflect human rights considerations that are relevant to its operations. For instance, in its safeguards policy, ADB sets out comprehensive requirements for addressing environmental and social risks and impacts, including a meaningful consultation process. The ADB Access to Information Policy has a presumption in favor of proactive information disclosure for transparency. The Accountability Mechanism provides an institutional response to grievance redressal ensuring compliance and accountability.

It is expected that the new Environmental and Social Framework (ESF) will provide further clarity on the environmental and social requirements at the project level and will strengthen the stakeholder engagement process and grievance mechanisms.

ADB continues to improve the implementation of the SPS through optimum understanding and the effectiveness of remedies. This translates human rights considerations into project requirements and strengthens ADB project environmental and social considerations under the ESF. Development of further guidance notes and implementation details explaining these project requirements to ADB staff and external implementation partners is recommended.

The ADB Accountability Mechanism office emphasizes meaningful participation with the conviction that it is important to engage with everyone, not leaving anyone behind. The mechanism must remain faithful to goals of transparency, independence, and accountability; be guided by openness, ethics, and justice; commit to treating people with dignity and respect; listen to stakeholders; and provide a forum for accountability, which is an essential feature of justice.

Construction site of the Viet Nam Central Mekong Delta Region Connectivity Project.
The project aims to improve connectivity and provide efficient access from Ho Chi Minh City to the Southern Coastal Region through the construction of two cable-stayed bridges across the Mekong River and associated roads (photo by ADB).

Revisiting Recommendations from 2016 and 2019 Accountability Mechanism Joint Learning Reports

To complement the forward-looking analysis geared toward system and process improvements, this report analyzes recommendations from past joint learning reports that have not been completed as of 2023. Unimplemented recommendations may result in a "relapse," or the recurrence of such complaints. System improvements implementing or operationalizing these recommendations are therefore needed. The ongoing SPS update may address the recommendations in this report. As the updated policy is being finalized, these recommendations are nevertheless reiterated here.

Box 7

Joint Learning Report Recommendations Implemented as of 2023

Enhanced Awareness Raising for Improved Implementation of the Accountability Mechanism Policy

The Accountability Mechanism offices—jointly, independently, or together with other internal and external partners—initiated several reforms to enhance development effectiveness of ADB through robust accountability. Initiatives include:

(i)   ADB adopted a new approach for enhanced awareness raising and capacity development by encouraging the CCSD and operations departments to organize joint learning sessions on the integrated function of the SPS and AMP, implementation challenges, and solutions learned from good practices. ADB organized detailed sessions with executing agencies, implementing agencies, CSOs, and ADB staff in India and the Philippines that were rated highly useful and—in the case of the Philippines learning event—acknowledged by ADB as a knowledge solution bank-wide.

(ii) Together with other MDB IAMs, the Accountability Mechanism offices reached out to CSOs in a few countries to share common Accountability Mechanism principles, procedures, and differences. The CSOs (that usually assist communities and affected persons) are better equipped to help people, especially in projects that are cofinanced by the MDBs.

(iii) ADB reactivated focal points in all resident missions and regional offices with detailed TORs. Specific training is planned for these focal persons.

(iv) OCRP conducted sessions with all regional departments, SPD, and OGC to share in-depth knowledge on the role and mandate of the Accountability Mechanism and its lessons learned.

continued on next page

Box 7 *continued*

(v)	The Accountability Mechanism offices and management have developed a 5-point action plan for improved implementation of ADB accountability: (a) strengthening of GRMs, (b) tracking of ineligible mechanism complaints handled by operations departments, (c) ensuring confidentiality of complainant identities and reducing the risk of reprisal, (d) ensuring early and effective information dissemination on the ADB Accountability Mechanism, and (e) the qualities of a good remedial action plan.

(vi)	To deal with persisting concerns of lack of awareness about the Accountability Mechanism amongst stakeholders, the Accountability Mechanism is working toward various awareness raising initiatives, including trying to get a loan covenant approved requiring the staff to provide simple and easy information about the mechanism's mandate and function at the earliest stages of their project conception. The covenant is to be accompanied by comprehensive language around the Accountability Mechanism in the project Administration Manual.

(vii)	The Accountability Mechanism offices published comprehensive learning reports based on the cases dealt with during 2016–2021. These reports serve as useful advice for required systemic reforms.

(viii)	As a member of the Independent Accountability Mechanism Network of several international organizations, the mechanism offices joined working groups on issues such as retaliation, governance, talent management, remedy, and outreach to ensure coordinated and greater efforts to address these issues. This work also facilitates cross-cultivating good practices.

ADB = Asian Development Bank; AMP = Accountability Mechanism Policy; CCSD = Climate Change and Sustainable Development Department; CSO = civil society organization; GRM = grievance redress mechanism; IAM = independent accountability mechanisms; MDB = multilateral development bank; OCRP = Office of the Compliance Review Panel; OGC = Office of the General Counsel; SPD = Strategy, Policy, and Partnerships Department; SPS = Safeguard Policy Statement; TORs = terms of reference.

Sources: 2016 Learning Report on the Implementation of the Accountability Mechanism Policy, 2019 Learning Report on Implementation of the Accountability Mechanism Policy.

Revisiting Recommendation 1: Strengthening Consultation and Participation

Both the 2016 and 2019 joint learning reports recommended the strengthening of consultation and participation in project design and implementation.

The 2016 Learning Report on the Implementation of the Accountability Mechanism Policy (the first joint learning report) states:

The review of the Accountability Mechanism cases shows that most of the complaints have listed a lack of adequate and meaningful consultation as a trigger. This has not changed over the past 12 years, and it continues to be an issue often underlying new complaints received by the operations departments. Deficiencies in information, consultation, and participation during project design and implementation have been raised as issues in almost all complaints. The affected persons have complained about not having been fully informed of their options in a way that enabled them to make informed decisions.[63]

The 2016 Joint Learning Report suggested that:

> [i]f meaningful consultations, which include improved information sharing, regular involvement, and communication with project beneficiaries, and resolving conflicts quickly, are carried out in a timely fashion, the probability of complaints should be less. Even if there is a complaint, chances are that it will be resolved faster because of the trust and respect built from regular consultation. With meticulous efforts to plug these deficiencies, the objectives of meaningful consultation will be achieved in coming years.[64]

The 2019 Learning Report on Implementation of the Accountability Mechanism Policy (second joint learning report) was summarized.

> In virtually all cases, the complaints have alleged inadequate consultation and participation. This was also one of the findings in a thematic evaluation study of ADB's safeguard implementation experience conducted by IED in 2016. The IED study indicated that ADB policy principles on meaningful consultation, disclosure, and GRM were not clearly understood by project-affected people. Many of the complaints to the [Accountability Mechanism] emerged during project implementation, and some have tended to fester because, by the time the complaint reaches the [Accountability Mechanism], the problem has become a source of frustration and irritation for the complainant.[65]

The 2019 Joint Learning Report noted that "[e]arly and more direct engagement might have reduced the scale and complexity of some complaints."[66]

Issues in consultation and communication persisted after the issuance of the joint learning reports. Analysis of these past joint learning reports—together with a review of all complaints received so far—show the depth of this issue. For instance, complaints filed as early as 2004 and until 2019 raised issues such as lack of meaningful consultation with affected persons, failure to communicate requirements for compensation to affected persons in advance causing the rejection of claims, lack of knowledge of affected persons of the GRM, inadequate consultation and information dissemination about a resettlement plan, and consultation efforts that did not adequately incorporate the views of affected persons.[67]

ADB must reinforce and execute the recommendations made in previous joint learning reports, as consultation can be considered a bedrock requirement whose absence has far-reaching consequences that impact all stages of the project.

---

[63] ADB. 2017. 2016 Learning Report on the Implementation of the Accountability Mechanism Policy. Manila.
[64] Footnote 63, p. 19.
[65] ADB. 2019. 2018 Learning Report on Implementation of the Accountability Mechanism Policy. Manila, p. 24 citing ADB. 2016. Real-Time Evaluation of ADB's Safeguard Implementation Experience Based on Selected Case Studies. Manila.
[66] Footnote 65, p. 25.
[67] Viet Nam CMDRCP, Georgia Batumi Road Project, Georgia Sustainable Urban Transport Project 1, Mongolia UUSGADIP 1, Cambodia Railway Project, CAREC Transport Corridor Project, Sri Lanka Transport Development Project, and India Mundra Power Project.

Despite several guarantees and requirements of meaningful consultations in the safeguards policies, the persistence of this issue requires systemic reform in various areas. These include (i) robust stakeholder mapping to ensure everyone affected by the project is consulted; (ii) provision of customized and holistic mitigation measures to adverse impacts; (iii) comprehensive due diligence of project impacts and discussion of such impacts with stakeholders in an efficient, need-based, and timely manner; and (iv) use of technology and innovation in providing remedies to ensure vulnerabilities are considered and addressed. These reforms could complement improvements in consultations brought about by the SPS update where ESS 9 on stakeholder engagement includes requirements for the preparation of stakeholder engagement plans.

Revisiting Recommendation 2: Improving the Project Grievance Redress Mechanisms

The improvement of the project grievance redress mechanism (GRM) was an overarching theme in the 2018 Joint Learning Report. It observed that "[i]n most of the AM cases over the last 3 years, the GRMs were not functioning well or were absent… In some cases, the GRM was not sufficiently operational at an early stage to address the issues."[68] The report noted that the functionality of a GRM is among the institutional causes and/or factors determining the effectiveness and efficiency with which complaints are resolved.[69]

OSPF recognized the importance of improving the effectiveness of project GRMs (based on problem-solving casework and tools and the demand for GRM training programs), and initiated knowledge and support technical assistance (TA) for Capacity Building for Grievance Redress and Dispute Resolution During Project Implementation.[70]

The TA project is intended to increase the efficiency and effectiveness of development projects, avoiding costs and delays in project implementation caused by the risk of complaints to the ADB Accountability Mechanism, and improving project sustainability. The TA project should improve the understanding and application of GRMs and the problem-solving performance of ADB DMC executing and implementing agencies and other key stakeholders such as civil society organizations.

The implementation of the TA project has been extended until 25 September 2023. As of April 2023, the project delivered 20 training and capacity development programs, including six virtual or hybrid sessions by OSPF across 12 ADB DMCs. These were in Bangladesh, Bhutan, Fiji, Georgia, India, Indonesia, Mongolia, Nepal, the Philippines, Sri Lanka, Uzbekistan, and Viet Nam. The coronavirus disease (COVID-19) pandemic disrupted planned TA activities that were largely to be held in person. This resulted in the need to shift to a virtual initiative with the use of online meeting platforms that were attended by more than 500 participants across sectors.

In 2020—despite the pandemic and lockdown—OSPF completed the development and launch of e-learning modules to supplement its capacity-building and training programs on GRMs (July) and problem-solving tools (October). In India, two Safeguard and Accountability Mechanism webinar series were conducted for resident mission staff and another for executing and implementing

---

[68]   Footnote 65, p. 25.
[69]   Footnote 65, p. 27.
[70]   ADB. 2018. Capacity Building for Grievance Redress and Dispute Resolution During Project Implementation. Manila.

government agencies for ADB-assisted projects. OSPF led the webinar series in collaboration with the Safeguards Division of SDCC, SARD, the India Resident Mission, and OCRP.

A webinar series was conducted in February 2021 for executing and implementing government agencies of ADB-assisted projects in the Philippines. OSPF also launched the OSPF Lessons Learned series documenting its complaint management experience. The TA project completed five case studies including two projects from Georgia, one from Mongolia, and two from Sri Lanka. GRM and problem-solving tools initiated through the TA project have been strengthened in part by these training programs.

A functioning and efficient GRM plays a crucial role in addressing grievances promptly to avoid escalation to the courts and Accountability Mechanism offices, and efforts need to continue. The 2021 Accountability Mechanism Annual Report recognized this, stating that the increasing trend in complaints filed is possibly due to ineffective GRMs.[71]

ADB must reiterate and reinforce the resolutions made in the 2019 Accountability Mechanism Annual Report, which focused on GRMs.[72] OCRP and OSPF have committed to strengthening the ADB Accountability Mechanism knowledge base through analytical work on project GRMs and lessons from case management. OSPF and OCRP will strive to remain relevant and provide advisory services through more targeted capacity-building and learning activities including eLearning on GRM, problem-solving, and certified mediation training.[73]

[71] ADB. 2022. Facilitating ADB In Operationalizing Its Core Values, Accountability Mechanism Annual Report. Manila.
[72] ADB. 2020. Enhancing Accountability and Project-Level Grievance Mechanisms, Accountability Mechanism Annual Report. Manila.
[73] Footnote 72, p. 36.

River siphon in the city of Bekasi, part of the Indonesia Integrated Citarum Water Resources Management Investment Program (ICWRMIP) Project 1. The ICWRMIP's objective is to improve water availability and improve integrated water resources management (photo by ADB).

Conclusion

Actions, solutions, and recommendations that came about through the Accountability Mechanism process have forged and reinforced the characteristics of good governance and contributed toward the development effectiveness of ADB through strengthened governance.

Participation and consensus building have been bolstered by the problem-solving process whereby OSPF facilitation enabled continuous dialogue and the building of trust between ADB and its stakeholders. One compliance review directly enhanced the rule of law, which triggered a gap analysis comparing ADB safeguards with national laws on land acquisition, aligning resettlement plans with both frameworks. Another compliance review uncovered shortcomings in the sharing of information on project changes to stakeholders, paving the way for increased transparency. The problem-solving process brought about prompt action on a project, which enabled a quick contractual agreement and successful closure of the case.

Findings of a lack of gender sensitivity in a project resulted in Board-approved recommendations for increased project attention to gender concerns, thereby strengthening inclusiveness. Efficiency—particularly from an environmental perspective—was enhanced due to findings of a lack of rigor in the review of impact assessments. Accountability—which is the essence of the Accountability Mechanism—was reinforced due to the consistency in requiring compliance with ADB safeguard and compliance requirements.

Accountability Mechanism systems and process improvements may be instituted in the future. For instance, robust due diligence helps minimize compliance issues and can lower costs of reparation, remedy, and reputational risk. Planning and management of human and financial resources—specifically for safeguarding and compliance—will aid project efficiency. The formulation of retaliation risk guidelines and assessment tools will enhance accountability and development effectiveness. Remedy escalation guidelines will aid accountability and efficiency, as will strengthening access to information, integrated safeguard monitoring, and standardized GRM processes.